No Ordinary Child:
Living Life in the Face of Autism

No Ordinary Child:
Living Life in the Face of Autism

DEBBIE WILSON

Copyright © 2019 by Debbie A. Wilson

ISBN: 978-0-9855532-4-1

All rights reserved. Except as permitted under the U.S. Copyright Act of 1976, no part of this publication may be reproduced, distributed, or transmitted in any form or by any means, or stored in a database or retrieval system, without the prior written permission of the publisher.

Scripture quotations marked (NIV) are taken from the Holy Bible, New International Version®, NIV®. Copyright © 1973, 1978, 1984, 2011 by Biblica, Inc. ™ Used by permission of Zondervan. All rights reserved worldwide. www.zondervan.com The "NIV" and "New International Version" are trademarks registered in the United States Patent and Trademark Office by Biblica, Inc. ™

Scripture quotations marked (NLT) are taken from the Holy Bible, New Living Translation, copyright ©1996, 2004, 2015 by Tyndale House Foundation. Used by permission of Tyndale House Publishers, Inc., Carol Stream, Illinois 60188. All rights reserved.

Scripture quotations marked (TLB) are taken from The Living Bible copyright © 1971. Used by permission of Tyndale House Publishers, Inc., Carol Stream, Illinois 60188. All rights reserved.

Front cover design by Lisa Hainline. Author photo by Margie Nielsen Photography. All other photos are from the author's collection.

Dedication

To Katelyn, who is the best little sister in the whole world

Contents

Chapter One 9
Chapter Two 17
Chapter Three 23
Chapter Four 33
Chapter Five 39
Chapter Six 47
Chapter Seven 55
Chapter Eight 77
Chapter Nine 95
Chapter Ten 111
Chapter Eleven 129
Chapter Twelve 137

A Note from Brittany 147
Excerpt from *Blessed Assurance*:
"Fighting the Good Fight" 151
Afterword 153
Photos 157
Acknowledgments 173
About the Author 175

Chapter One

"Hey guys, would you come outside with me for a minute? There's something I think you'll want to see."

In the waiting room at the occupational therapy center, Todd and I put aside the magazines we'd been reading and followed Melissa, Brittany's therapist, down the hall and out the back. The yard featured a large, fenced-in area with swings and other playground equipment. Through the middle ran a narrow, paved pathway that began at the back fence and ended at the door where we now stood.

"We have a surprise for you. Something we've been working on for quite some time." Melissa motioned to Brittany, who was standing beside a bicycle at the path's far end. "Go ahead, girl!" she called. "Show them what you can do."

Brittany swung one leg over the bar of the bike and placed her foot on a pedal. She pushed off with the other foot and began pedaling. She looked a little unsteady at first, but she confidently gained her balance and continued forward.

"Look at you, Brittany!" I yelled. "You are *doing* it!" I fought back tears as she rode all the way up to us.

Todd hugged her as she dismounted. "You put your mind to it, and you did it!"

Brittany had been wanting to get to this point for years, but lack of balance and coordination had prevented her from mastering the bicycle. She'd watch as Katelyn, her younger sister, coasted up and down our long gravel driveway and ask, "When do you think I can ride like that, Mama? I'm ten, and she's only eight."

"You are riding a bike, Britt."

"No, I mean ride without training wheels."

"You will, one day." I saw her determination, knew she was intent on accomplishing her goal, yet in the back of my mind I wondered if she really would be able. Many children learn to ride by or before age six, and most before eight; she would soon turn eleven.

This may seem a relatively small feat, but for us it was huge. While Brittany had faced innumerable developmental delays since her birth, once again we were relieved and delighted to see that her hard work and resolve had helped her to reach another milestone.

Our firstborn, who brought such joy to our lives, would give us many more moments of triumph in the years to come. Todd and I hadn't had kids right away. Though I'd wanted to start a family shortly after we married, persuading Todd that it was the right time took several years. Whenever we talked about it, he would remind me that real life doesn't always mirror our dreams.

I wasn't sure why he seemed always to worry that we might have a child with special needs. This was foreign to me; it had never really crossed my mind. Even so, it was having an impact on him.

"My parents had four healthy babies, and your parents had two," I remember saying. "Why are you so concerned about something being wrong with our baby?"

"I don't really know why I've thought about it, but I have."

It was on a Sunday that I finally convinced him.

We'd finished church services and were heading home for lunch.

"Any thoughts on what the preacher said today?"

"Hmm—from which part of the sermon?"

"I'm thinking of when he quoted Jesus, from the verses in Matthew, about how the birds don't worry about what they'll eat, and the lilies don't worry about how they'll be clothed. And about how, in God's care, these are even more beautiful than all of Solomon's attire. I know it's difficult not to worry about tomorrow. I know you're worried that a baby might change what we have now as a couple, but I think it will make what we have even better."

Todd agreed, and this was the turning point. From that day forward we both wanted the same thing, a baby. It was also the beginning of a frustration that would creep its way into our lives: the frustration of not being able to get pregnant.

Every month I'd get my hopes up, only to see them dashed. Months turned into years, and there were many days I felt like the barren Hannah, Elkanah's wife, who for so long yearned to have a child. When she went to the Lord's house to pray for a baby, Hannah made a vow to Him, that if He were willing to give her a son, she would dedicate the child to His service. I could relate to this woman's desperate prayer.

Todd and I had been married six years, and by now we'd been trying to conceive for at least two. Month after month I would pray that the pregnancy test would come back positive; month upon month the result proved disappointing.

Finally, I came to a crossroads. May had arrived, school was out soon, and I resolved not to spend the entire summer off from my teaching position worried. I prayed, affirming that God's timing, whatever it was, would be best, and I stopped letting *have a baby!* consume my every waking moment.

Days and then weeks began going by quickly. Todd would leave for work each morning before daylight, usually before I awakened, to drive a tractor on the farm until dark. My days were consumed with helping my sister Amy finish the preparations for her upcoming wedding. Dress fittings, decorations, and so on—and then the wedding itself—filled up the month of June.

On the first morning in July I woke craving a big breakfast. Walking to the refrigerator for eggs, I glanced at the calendar on its door. It was still showing June, so I flipped the page to display the new month. As soon as I clipped the holding magnet back into place, I glimpsed a handwritten note in the July 1 box: "P Test." My eyes went wide. I'd forgotten about the monthly reminders I'd added to indicate if my cycle was late.

My eyes grew wider still with the thought: *pregnancy is a possibility.* "Lord, could it really be happening?" I knew now that, though always regular, I was more than a week late. Flying to the back of the house, I started rummaging through the bathroom cabinet, throwing aside lotions and towels. I always kept a test in reserve, yet after a thorough search I couldn't find one.

The decision to redirect my focus at the end of the school year had proven effective. I hadn't even realized I'd used the last test. Fumbling my way back out to the couch, I sat and with nervous excitement closed my eyes, took a deep breath, and began to pray.

"I know your timing is always perfect, but, Lord, I can't help myself. I am praying that this is your perfect time for us to start a family. I'm praying that you will answer our prayers and give us a child. Please, let me be pregnant. We want a baby so badly. If this isn't the time, show me how to be content in knowing that you know what's best for us, because your will is the most important thing in our lives."

Opening my eyes, I decided in a split second that instead of heading to the store for another test, I would get ready and go straight to my OB/GYN's office. I practically leaped off the couch toward the bath. Dressed and ready to go within thirty minutes, I sat on the bed to put on my shoes.

My mind, no longer in the present, was contemplating how I'd break the wonderful news to Todd if the test came back positive. I weighed several different plans as I hopped up and gathered my purse and keys. One scenario after another had me smiling as I walked out the door.

Chapter Two

I APPROACHED THE RECEPTIONIST'S window where Carolyn, a friend from church, was seated at her desk behind the glass.

"Good morning!"

She looked up from her computer. "Well, good morning. You don't have an appointment today, do you?"

"No." I beamed. "I don't have an appointment."

"Doctor Ziegler hasn't even made it in, he's still doing rounds at the hospital. Anyway, why are you here so early—and why are you all smiles?"

"Do you think I could have a pregnancy test done?"

"Sure! Do you think you need one?"

"I think so."

"I can definitely help you with that. Come on to the back."

Carolyn gave me some instructions, I did the test, and we waited. Then she looked up suddenly and grinned. "It's positive—a very slight positive, but positive."

I squealed and reached over to hug her neck. "A slight positive is still *positive*!" I could barely contain my elation. I wanted to shout the news to the whole world. "Okay. Carolyn, promise me you won't tell a soul. Promise! Todd won't be home until tonight, and I want to tell him and the family first."

"I won't say a word. I promise." She hugged me again, and we both giggled.

On the drive home I began playing out some of the scenarios I'd pondered earlier, before leaving home. I couldn't decide how I'd tell Todd that he was finally going to be a father. I considered buying a little tractor and putting it on the counter for him to see as he came through the door. He would ask me about it, and I would say that we'd needed to make sure our little boy knew all about farm equipment. I considered getting a pair of baby shoes and putting them on the dresser, so he'd see them during the routine of emptying all his pockets before getting into the shower.

Ideas were still bouncing around my mind when I pulled into the driveway and parked. I switched off the ignition, and in that quiet moment I realized: in all my excitement I had forgotten to thank God for answering yes to my prayer. I bowed my head, and the words began to pour out.

"O God, you are so merciful. You know my heart. Thank you so much for the gift of a child, just as you gave us the gift of your own Son, thousands of years ago. I pray for a healthy child we can nurture and love. I promise to share your promises and your love with our baby. More than anything else, Lord, I want this baby I am carrying to come to know you in a personal way just as we have in our own lives."

Waiting for Todd all afternoon and beyond was pure torture. I wanted to race out to the farm with the good news but knew finding him would be no simple task—there were too many fields to search through, on hundreds of acres. I had to be content to wait, so I went into the kitchen and started making a celebratory dinner. Unable to choose between the other ideas, I made up my mind to let him guess at the occasion for his favorite meal.

I was pouring up tea when I heard the truck on the driveway. I thought my heart would beat right out of my chest! Keys rattled in the door, and then it swung open.

Todd grinned at me as he walked in, covered from head to toe with dust. "Hey, little mama."

I smiled back. "Why did you call me that?"

"Call you what?"

"You said, 'Hey, little mama.'"

"I don't know. It's just a figure of speech."

I locked my eyes with his. "No, it's not. Not anymore."

"What?"

My smile nearly reached my ears as I shook my head. Todd enveloped me in a hug.

We both knew our lives were about to change. We went to bed that night too animated to sleep, so we tossed around baby names until the early morning hours. I was convinced we were going to have a boy, and I wanted to name him Matthew after my great-grandfather.

"What if it isn't a boy? You better pick out some girl names too, Debbie, just in case."

I began scanning the book of names that I'd bought. "What about Brooke?"

By now Todd was reading another book. He peeked across the top and said, "I like Brittany."

"I like the name 'Brittany' too. Let me look up its

meaning." I quickly flipped pages. "Here it is—this book says, 'from Britain.' The meaning isn't that special, but I still like the name. What middle name would go with it?"

"Elizabeth is a pretty name. What does that mean?"

I flipped forward to the E section. "It means 'oath of God.' Brittany Elizabeth Wilson—I like it!"

When I rolled over and closed my eyes, I went to sleep with a grateful heart, thankful for God's answers to our prayers.

※

The nine months I carried Brittany were better than I could have possibly imagined. Initially there were the usual few weeks of morning sickness, but other than a little nausea my pregnancy went smoothly. About halfway along, through an ultrasound, we learned we were having a girl. While I hadn't seen it coming, we were both ecstatic; hearing her heartbeat and seeing her tiny hands and feet filled us with an undescribable joy.

Picking out baby clothes, bedding, and even her first few toys were incredible experiences. I read *What to Expect When You're Expecting*, *Your Pregnancy Week by Week,* and seemingly every other relevant book I could find, wanting to make sure I did everything "right." Before she was born, I read, sang, and talked to her daily so she would know how much I loved her.

Several weeks before my due date our church gave me a baby shower, and I was more excited than ever as I opened gifts of tiny clothes. When we placed everything in her nursery that night, I could feel Brittany kicking as if she likewise were thrilled by her new presents. As I laid out each little outfit in her bed, I smiled, thinking about dressing her up. I wanted the remaining weeks to pass quickly so I could hold her in my arms.

Not long thereafter, Todd and I attended a childbirth class at the hospital where Brittany would be delivered. We learned so much, and as we sat in the meeting room with other first-time parents, hearing about the typical phases of labor and delivery, I think Todd could sense that I was getting a bit nervous about the birth.

When the nurse asked about our hopes, I said, "I just want her to be healthy." Todd joked, "I'm just hoping for a quiet child." In the days to come, we would discover that neither of these wishes would come true.

Chapter Three

EARLY ON THE Monday of March 11, 1991, about a week before Brittany was due, my water broke. I knew from childbirth classes that labor now would need to be induced. We saw Dr. Ziegler a few hours before noon, and after an exam at his clinic he directed me to pack a bag and head to the hospital, where he would meet us and get started. This already wasn't going to resemble the perfect delivery I'd hoped for during the last nine months.

I labored through the afternoon and through the evening, but as I'd made no progress Dr. Ziegler decided a Cesarean was necessary. I didn't even remember C-section being mentioned in our class—I'd surely tuned out the instructors, thinking it wouldn't apply to me. In pure panic mode, and asked to sign the consent forms, I also realized the pain was more intense than the panic. Todd put on blue scrubs and a cap, prepping to join me, yet following a failed epidural we were told I'd be put under for the procedure, so he couldn't be in the delivery room for Brittany's birth.

"It's going to be all right," he said. "I promise." He gave me a kiss as the nurses began wheeling me away.

The hospital hallway was lined with friends and family, and after much anticipation Brittany Elizabeth Wilson was born at 12:59 a.m. on Tuesday, March 12, 1991. Her every moment and movement were caught on video as she was carried to the nursery, weighed, and checked for all her first vital signs. Everyone was crowded together to peer through the glass window, some joking about who she resembled, as a nurse placed her on the scales.

Mama said, "She sure doesn't look like Debbie did at birth—she was practically bald. Look at that full head of dark hair!"

Nurses poked and prodded while everyone awaited the announcement. The nursery door finally opened: Brittany was 7 pounds 8 ounces, and a little over twenty inches long. Todd beamed with pride as he stared at his gorgeous little girl; my heart melted later, when the nurses brought her so that I could hold her for the first time. All I wanted was to have her with me and to stare at her lovely face. After a few minutes, though, one nurse said she needed to be taken back to the nursery.

It had been a stressful day, and we were both exhausted, so we relented without protest and let her go. Todd sat next to me on the bed, leaned down, and kissed me. "She's beautiful."

I looked into his eyes. "She's perfect."

The nurse returned with a pillow and a blanket so Todd could be reasonably comfortable on the bedside foldout chair. She smiled and turned off the light on her way out, and we both fell quickly asleep.

The next morning, I woke to the beeping of my IV. Looking over and seeing Todd reading in the chair, I grinned as I tried to shake off haze and fog from the medications.

"Do you think it's too early to ask the nurse to bring the baby?"

He put down the newspaper and handed me the call button. "Only one way to find out."

The moment I pressed the signal, a voice came through the speaker. "May I help you?"

"Yes, can you bring my baby to the room for a little while?"

"I'll be right there."

I was surprised when the nurse entered without Brittany in her arms. She certainly saw my disappointment.

"I wanted to let you know that Dr. Gates has just completed the baby's first pediatric exam. He will be here in just a few minutes to talk with you."

I don't know if it was the tone of her voice or a mother's instinct, but I got a sinking feeling in my stomach. She left, and when the door opened again, Dr. Gates walked over and sat in the big wooden rocker in the room's corner. Even in the very dim light I could see his silver hair and his smile. He placed his hands on both arms of the chair and leaned forward.

We'd chosen Dr. Gates on the recommendation of friends with young children; many of them mentioned his wonderful bedside manner. We'd met him about a month before, when we went to his office to sign papers so he could be our baby's pediatrician. I remembered now his kind demeanor as he re-introduced himself, yet behind the pleasantries I read concern on his face and became more uneasy.

"Mr. and Mrs. Wilson, I just finished a thorough

exam of Brittany, and she is still somewhat lethargic. The nurses also have told me that she's having some feeding problems."

I pulled myself to an upright position. I didn't understand. "What does that mean, Dr. Gates? What do you mean by 'still lethargic'?"

"Dr. Ziegler indicated that when Brittany was born, she showed some signs of being what we call a 'floppy baby.' Initially she had a low Apgar score—that rating scale shows how a baby is doing immediately after delivery. He did say the score improved within a few minutes.

"What I'm a little concerned about now is that she isn't eating as well as we would like her to, and she doesn't seem to be able to keep her milk down. I want to keep her in the nursery for a day so the nurses can monitor her closely."

At this point I stayed silent, not knowing how to respond.

Todd spoke up. "Dr. Gates, is this something serious?"

"Well, because of the problems at birth, if her feeding issues don't improve significantly by tomorrow morning, I want to send her to the neonatal unit at the hospital downtown and let them run some tests.

"However, I'm sure everything will be fine. Mrs.

Wilson, get some rest, and I'll be back again to talk with you more in the morning."

When the doctor had gone, Todd sat down on the bed beside me, and I fell into his arms, crying. I thought he might say, "This is why I wasn't sure about having kids. This is the very reason I wanted it to stay just the two of us." Instead he held me and whispered, "It's going to be fine, babe. Don't cry. Everything is going to be all right."

I slept through the remainder of the day but had difficulty that night. I felt consumed by restlessness, and my pain wasn't associated with the C-section. It was heartache for my baby girl.

By Thursday morning, awaiting Dr. Gates, I was nothing but nervous energy. As the nurse was checking my vitals, he walked in and sat in the same corner rocking chair. When she removed the blood pressure cuff and moved away, I could see him, and I did not like his expression. I thought I saw tears in his eyes, and I teared up instantly. Todd had been asleep on the couch, but now he quickly came and sat next to me.

"I wish I had better news for you both this morning. But I'm afraid Brittany is still having feeding problems. The nurses placed her in the Level II nursery last night. One of them thinks she had a small seizure—she saw her eyes roll back."

I could tell that Dr. Gates genuinely was distressed over having to deliver this report. Already visibly upset, I began to cry, and Todd held my hand to comfort me while the doctor explained that the nurses would bring Brittany so we could see her before they placed her into the ambulance for the trip across town.

I blurted out, "Can we go with her?"

"Dr. Ziegler will have to release you first. The hospital usually allows new parents to stay close to the unit for a few days. I'll see what I can do to get you a room."

Again, I could tell he was troubled. After we'd sat in silence for a few moments, he stood.

Todd reached out to shake his hand and said, as he took his leave, "We appreciate what you're doing for us, Dr. Gates."

I sat frozen for some time, staring into space, beneath a heavy despair. There was nothing that could describe the anguish; neither of us had any words. We both were in shock as we waited to see our baby. Within a single day we'd gone from soaring jubilation to overwhelming heartbreak.

The nurse wheeled in Brittany so we could say our

goodbyes. I peeped into the clear-plastic bassinet and saw her beautiful blue eyes gazing back at me. She was so alert; her stare was penetrating. She looked like a healthy baby. Tears started pouring down my cheeks.

The nurse put her hand on my shoulder. "I'm sorry, we need to go ahead and bring her to the ambulance. It's waiting."

Todd and I watched as they wheeled her out and then down the hallway. Then he whispered, "I'm going to walk with them. I'll be back in a few minutes. I promise."

My emotions were raw. I turned back to the bed, alone. I buried my head in a pillow and sobbed.

"Why, God? This is not supposed to be happening. Please, Lord, take care of her. Please be with my baby."

I slowly rose and began getting dressed. The nurse came in, immediately displeased to see me up and moving without assistance, but I was so focused on my child that I ignored her concern. "Do you know when Dr. Ziegler will be here to release me?"

"Should be shortly, but you really need to get back into bed until then."

"I'm fine. I want to be ready to go as soon as he's here."

Todd returned and told me the ambulance had

departed. Dr. Gates must have reached Dr. Ziegler by phone and told him about Brittany's transfer downtown, because he had our discharge papers ready to sign when he arrived. While Todd went to get the car, I placed a pillow over my stomach to alleviate ache from the surgery and waited for the nurse to bring a wheelchair.

This was not how I'd envisioned leaving the hospital. The backseat's pink and gray baby seat was as empty as the void in my heart. *How can we go and not have our little girl?*

I stared through the window as we drove, praying the entire way. There was a familiarity to my pain—it was the type I'd experienced when my sister, Kathy, was murdered—a pain like no other. This was the pain of grief. I hadn't felt this way in ten years, and I had no idea that soon these two devastating experiences would interconnect in a very unexpected way.

Chapter Four

Todd found a convenient parking spot and acquired another wheelchair. No sooner had he brought me in than a nurse approached quickly.

"Are you the Wilsons?"

"Yes—has something happened?"

"I've just come from Neonatal—Dr. Desoler needs to meet with you right away. One of the nurses thinks your baby has had another seizure; you'll need to sign some consent forms for treatment."

Rather than being anxious I felt nearly crushed underneath sorrow. But Todd sped me through the halls behind the fast-stepping nurse. At the unit she showed us how to wash our hands and put on scrubs, which were required for any entry. After she punched a code into a wall keypad, double doors slowly opened to a large room featuring a host of sights and sounds that began spiking my anxiety.

Nurses tended to babies. Parents huddled beside little beds positioned in cubbyholes against the walls. A workstation bustled at the room's center. Doctors looked down at and then up from charts, giving instructions. Continuous beeping from the everywhere-present equipment, coupled with all the tubes running into and out of the tiniest bodies, threatened to shove me into a panic attack.

Brittany was sound asleep, on her back. I almost didn't recognize her amid all the tubes. The nurse could see my rising worry.

"I know it's not easy to take in all of this, but we are going to help your baby. We've started an IV and inserted a feeding tube that will give Brittany the nutrition she needs. We've also started her on phenobarbital, as an anti-seizure treatment. And the doctor will be here shortly to talk with you."

My head was spinning. I was thankful to be in a wheelchair. The sight of my child among those countless tubes nauseated and weakened me.

As the nurse walked away I eased up out of the chair and held on to the bed containing little Brittany.

She looked perfect with her head full of dark hair and beautiful porcelain skin. Todd held me around the waist. Nothing could have prepared us for the love we already felt for the baby I'd carried thirty-nine weeks.

As we stared into the crib, focused on our firstborn, we heard a voice: "Don't be scared to touch her."

I turned around to see a lady in a rocking chair, by a bed that cradled an almost impossibly small baby. "I was afraid too, in the beginning," she went on. "But it's important that she feel your touch."

I managed a smile as I resumed staring at Brittany. I wanted her eyes to open so I again could see the piercing blue she'd shown me before being taken in the ambulance. Her sleep was heavy, though, from the anti-seizure medication.

Then I heard another voice, this one male. I turned to see a tall thin man in a white lab coat. "Mr. and Mrs. Wilson, I'm Dr. Desoler. I'll be Brittany's primary physician here in Neonatal."

Todd responded for us. "Doctor, can you tell us what's wrong with Brittany? Did she have a seizure?"

"Some of our nurses saw her eyes roll to the back of her head as they were positioning her in the crib. With the chart history from the other hospital saying their nurses also saw this type of occurrence, we felt it best to put Brittany on a low dose of phenobarbital—that's an anti-seizure medication. If we don't see any other signs of seizures, we will slowly wean her off, over the next few days."

"What do you think is causing her feeding problems?"

"We're not sure, but we're going to do our best to discover the cause. We'll run some tests today to get to the bottom of the issues. I will be back around in the morning to discuss the results with you. The nurse will give you some information about the unit's four different visiting times, and I'll check back with you during one of those."

As Dr. Desoler walked to the nurses' station to fill out paperwork, I realized I hadn't made a sound, hadn't said a word—I knew if I had I couldn't have held back the tears. My heart was in a million pieces. I wanted to hold my baby, rock her in my arms and sing the lullabies I'd sung to her over the last nine months. Most of all I wanted to wake from this nightmare.

I knew that Christians are not immune to pain and sickness. I knew that God has never promised us our lives will be perfect here on earth. Even so, the sorrow was so overwhelming, it almost seemed too much to bear.

When I'd mourned Kathy's death, I leaned heavily

on the peace of knowing that God was with me. The grief I felt now as I gazed at my child, helpless in her crib, sent me running right into the arms of my Savior. I closed my eyes and began to pray silently.

"Please be with Brittany. Help the doctors as they try to find what is causing her problems. Most of all, Lord, help us to know that all things are possible if we have faith."

As I opened my eyes, someone said, "I know you're both scared. I was scared too when my daughter was first placed in the unit."

Again someone was offering encouragement. I turned and saw a lady holding a pen. She was young; her hair fell in soft black curls. She'd been writing in a small notebook on her lap.

"I know how difficult this is for you. Trust me. I know what you're feeling. Make sure you get a journal and write in it, every day. Write what the doctors tell you about the progress of your baby."

She spoke from experience, as I would discover. Her baby had been there many weeks.

I was so distraught over the entire situation I could barely think straight, with no belief that I'd be able to formulate thoughts to write down. I did manage another smile, and a thank-you.

Despite my skepticism, what the woman said did bring some calm to my heart. And, while I had no clue about it then, she and I shared a bond—a bond that no two people would want to have.

As I wrote about in *Sweet Scent of Justice* (2012), within eighteen months between 1980 and 1982, three girls were murdered in the same area. My sister was one of those three. After her death, we received a letter from a woman who also had lost her sister, in the same tragic way, just eight months before Kathy was killed. She truly understood our grief and invited us to call upon her if we wanted or needed to talk with someone.

This young woman, rocking and journaling about her own baby in the neonatal unit, was the very same woman who'd tragically lost her own sister and who had written that letter, ten years earlier.

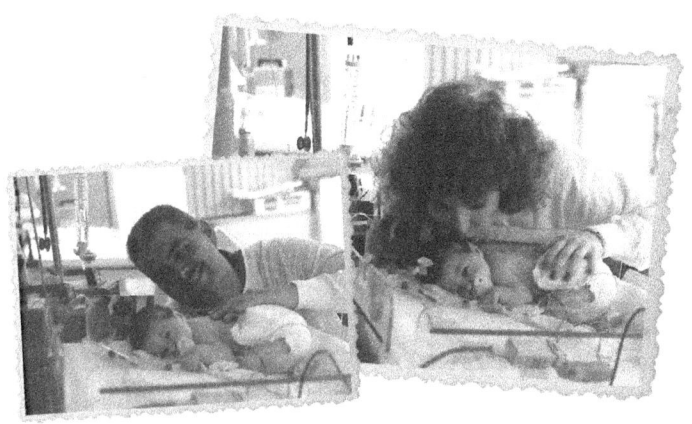

Chapter Five

WITH BRITTANY STILL in 24/7 care at the unit, twenty miles away, we settled for a time into a different kind of pattern. Todd would head home from the farm to pick me up, and we'd go together into the city to be with our baby. We followed this routine for weeks.

At the overpass just before the hospital exit, butterflies would flutter, and nausea would menace my stomach as I anticipated hearing the details of Brittany's condition. Over and over the news was the same: there were no answers as to why she couldn't hold down milk. Instead of gaining, she began to lose weight.

Gradually I lost weight too; I simply couldn't eat. Frequently I'd read verses like "Blessed are those who mourn, for they will be comforted" (Matthew 5:4 niv). I knew the Lord's presence could bring me peace far beyond my understanding, and often I asked that He would heal Brittany's little body so we could bring her home.

Every night at the house, passing by the door of the nursery we'd painted pink to match the crib's cream and pink bedding, I'd cry out to God: "I want to believe that your plan is always best for me. But Lord, I don't see how this could be best for any of us. Please make her well. You gave us such a blessing; please don't take this precious gift away from us."

I knew my only true comfort would come from Him. Yet my faith needed to be deepened. I felt indescribably troubled, and as vulnerable as I had after losing Kathy. Both were incomprehensible to me: as with how my sister could have been allowed to face what she endured, I didn't have a clue why our family should suffer so, once again.

As a child I had prayed and asked God to forgive my sins, welcomed Jesus as my Savior, and invited His Spirit into my heart to be my Lord. He had never left me through my grief when Kathy was murdered, and I knew He cared about the hurt I was feeling now. I marked John 16:33, where Jesus says, "Here on earth you will have many trials and sorrows. But take heart, because I have overcome the world" (nlt). I read this again and again and again, whenever I thought pain might literally burst my heart.

My parents and Todd's parents were there with Brittany at the unit during other visitation times. Neonatal allowed four one-hour visits a day, and when we weren't at the hospital the nurses allowed me to call and receive updates. One night I was told the IV had come out of Brittany's hand, and the only place they were able to put it back was into a vein on her head. To do that, though, they'd had to shave off all her beautiful hair. I cried just thinking about it. The nurses were wonderful, yet I wanted the whole nightmare to end, and this news only brought more grief.

Each time we talked with Brittany's doctor, nothing had changed and none of the tests had yielded any definitive answers. Thankfully, there were no more seizure episodes, so her phenobarbital dose was slowly decreased. And once she was completely weaned off the medicine her feeding tube was removed; she started to take small amounts of formula throughout the day. Over the course of several weeks she began to tolerate feedings, and eventually her daily amount started to increase. As her feeding problems slowly settled, she began to gain weight. This development buoyed our hopes, and we gave thanks.

One evening, when we arrived, I went straight to Brittany's bed, and she wasn't there. My heart began to race, but quickly scanning the room, I saw a nurse in a rocking chair with an infant, wrapped in a blanket, drinking from a small bottle. I felt such relief when I realized it was Brittany, swaddled up with no tubes attached.

The nurse grinned. "Are you ready to hold your baby?"

"*Yes!*" Tears of joy rolled down my face as I took Brittany and held her in my arms for the first time since the day she was born.

Dr. Desoler approached, smiling as he opened her chart. "Well, we took out the feeding tube. She's drinking on her own in small amounts—and keeping down the milk. I think we can say that whatever issues she experienced at birth are slowly being resolved."

I knew in my heart that God had resolved those difficulties. Just as He was sustaining us, He had taken care of her. I held our precious gift tightly.

We would need to stay one night in a private room with Brittany before she could be discharged. It was crucial that we feel comfortable about taking care of her on our own. We were taught, for instance, how to give an infant CPR, how to record the amount of formula at each feeding, and how to hook up the heart monitor she would wear for the next few weeks.

It was the day after Easter when at last we placed Baby Brittany into that pink and gray car seat. I sat in the back and don't think I ever looked away from her the entire drive. When she gazed at me with her big blue eyes, it seemed as though *she* realized that she was finally going home.

As we turned down the driveway, we could see a big pink bow on the tree in front of the house and a "Welcome Home, Brittany!" sign. Great-grandparents, grandparents, all her aunts and uncles, and her baby cousin greeted her. That was one of the happiest days of my life, and our love for our daughter would grow each day. My faith had been strengthened already through the difficulties, and it would continue to be tested during the trials that were to come.

Plainly, our arrival home was across-the-board different from what I'd envisioned during the days of pregnancy. Instead of wanting to feed and bathe my baby girl, I was scared to touch her. Todd bathed her and fed her during the first few days until I came to trust that she wasn't going to break.

The hospital set up weekly visits with different doctors to continue monitoring Brittany's progress. On one of the first, we were told that during the multitude of tests they'd discovered she was born with hip bones not fully aligned in their sockets; they needed to fit her for a brace. She was still a newborn. While in a way this did seem a trivial thing after the weeks of not knowing if our baby would live or die, nevertheless, when the doctor began placing her tiny legs into the contraption, I began to get very emotional.

Todd holding Brittany in her brace

"Are you all right, Mrs. Wilson? This will limit her movement, yes, but I promise—it doesn't hurt her at all." A technician adjusted the little straps and tightened the brace to fit her legs.

"I know," I faltered. "It just... it doesn't look very comfortable."

We were able to take it off for baths, but otherwise she had to wear it day and night. She bore this burden for several months until her X-rays showed that the hip bones were in their normal position.

As a young mother, I struggled to accept that a tiny little baby should have to withstand such trials. I wasn't prepared for the feelings and emotions brought on by my own child's pain and suffering. I couldn't get my mind around how God could love me enough to have watched His own Son suffer just for me.

When Brittany was in the neonatal intensive care unit, I'd often thought about the biblical story of Samuel. I knew that Hannah, his barren mother, had prayed continuously for a baby and made a vow to give her child back to the Lord if He would bless her with a son. After Samuel's birth she kept her promise, and when he was old enough she took him to the tabernacle and entrusted him to Eli so he could devote his life to serving God.

I also made promises to God when I prayed and asked Him to give me a child. I too promised to offer my baby back to Him for His service. Once she was born, I couldn't imagine giving her up in the way that Hannah had surrendered Samuel.

After God answered our prayers and Brittany's issues at birth were resolved, I understood that He must have a very special plan for her life. My prayer was that He would use her life in whatever way He chose, just as He used Samuel's, for His glory.

Chapter Six

I WAS ELATED WHEN Brittany began meeting all the month-by-month expectations for her age. She rolled over, smiled, sat without support, and hit every other target on the developmental chart Dr. Gates had given us.

At the neonatal unit Dr. Desoler had suggested that, given her initial complications, we take Brittany to a pediatric neurologist before she turned one. When she reached nine months, we traveled to Children's Hospital New Orleans, where Dr. Willis evaluated her. We were anxious, because doctors who'd cared for Brittany during her first several weeks had been concerned about possible neurological issues. We were relieved, then, by the diagnosis that she was perfectly healthy.

Dr. Willis didn't have more specific answers for us, yet he was reassuring: "While I can't explain what happened at her birth, I can tell you Brittany is a neurologically and intellectually intact child." Dr. Gates had been giving us good progress reports, yes, but a second positive opinion, and from a specialist, made this seem more "official."

Brittany continued to meet regular milestones: making sounds, crawling, and then soon transitioning from taking a few steps on her first birthday to walking. When she wasn't toddling to and fro, she was climbing into my lap with a book for me to read to her.

She somehow seemed to understand every word, even when the books were advanced for her. I would ask questions about the story, and she would point to the characters, always knowing the answers. She was such a happy baby, full of curiosity and energy. By then the shaved hair was a distant memory—she had full, beautiful auburn curls. Her big blue eyes were surrounded with eyelashes so thick they appeared covered with mascara.

Our days were full of laughter and play. Conversely, during the ever-challenging nights Brittany wiggled and squirmed, fiercely resisting sleep. The only way she didn't fuss was if I rocked and sang to her. She would bury her face in my long hair and inhale to smell it, over and over. Then she would play with it, listening intently to the songs until at long last she would drift off. Music drew her attention and calmed her.

Brittany looking through one of her many books

At fifteen months she loved to watch her video of Mother Goose songs and rhymes while trying to sing along and dancing around the room.

At twenty-one months she could talk well enough to tell us what she wanted as well as repeat the words we said to her. When we found out I was expecting our second child, I couldn't wait to share the news to see how she would react.

"Brittany, you are going to be a big sister."

"Big sister," she repeated, reaching up her arms for me to lift her. I kissed her cheek and hugged her tightly. She didn't show any emotion but kept saying the words again and again. "Big sister. Big sister. Big sister."

Todd and I were excited, but at the same time we were a little anxious about the pregnancy. What if it happened again? I couldn't fathom enduring the same type of experience twice. I prayed that God would grant us a healthy baby. And I became a bit fearful of how Brittany would respond to what we had learned would be a second baby girl. "Todd, how do you think Brittany will act around a little sister? She's such a mama's girl that I'm scared she'll be jealous."

"I think she will be fine."

"Let's go ahead and pick out a baby name, so we can begin preparing her. I'm not sure how you'd feel about this… but I've been thinking about naming the baby after Kathy."

"Your sister Kathy?"

"Yes. Well, it wouldn't need to be that exact name—I like Katelyn, though." I walked to the shelf, reached for the book with baby names, and thumbed through. "Katelyn means 'pure,' or 'perfect.' I love it! What do you think?"

"I'm fine with that. What about Victoria for her middle name?"

"Katelyn Victoria… it's perfect!"

Via planned C-section, a fully healthy Katelyn Victoria entered the world four days after Christmas 1992. Her name fit: she was perfect in every way.

We stayed just two nights in the hospital, following which we were overjoyed to place Katelyn into the pink and gray baby seat and take her home with us.

Brittany on a pallet with Katelyn

Katelyn came into our lives just as her big sister entered her terrible twos. Completely mobile, Brittany seemed to run on an endless energy supply. She didn't slow down from the moment her eyes popped open in the morning until she could not fight sleep for another second at night. She required very little rest, and there were many nights we put her between us in our bed so we could get some sleep and she wouldn't hurt herself trying to climb up over the edge of her crib.

Brittany loved her baby sister and always wanted to hold her. I would let her sit in my lap to hold Katelyn, but I had to watch her constantly because she always wanted to handle her like one of her dolls. She didn't understand that she could hurt her. She thought it was fun to yank Katelyn's bottle or pacifier from her mouth and race off to another room while laughing hysterically. I'd heard quite a lot about this toddler stage, so the behavior and energy didn't seem to me out of the ordinary.

She loved to laugh, and she took any chance she got to agitate her sister or her cousins. For instance, she found it riotously funny to coax them into a big box they were playing with and then hold the lid shut while they shouted to get out.

"Brittany, you march yourself right to that chair

and sit there until you decide to be nice to Jodi, Bradi, and Katelyn."

"I'll be good! I'll be good!"

She always promised to act differently, but she spent a lot of time in that chair thinking about how to do so. She had absolutely no patience for waiting her turn, and she'd pitch a fit to get her way. After a day of chasing her, I would lie in bed at night hearing "I'll be sweet, I'll be sweet" in my head until I drifted off to sleep.

The first sign of developmental issues came when we brought Brittany in for another round of her vaccinations. Dr. Gates had moved to another state; a new pediatrician had taken over his practice, and this was our first visit. Right away, a nurse came in and gave the shots, and Brittany began to cry inconsolably. When the doctor entered the room a short time later, Brittany began clinging to me, climbing up my chest, and squeezing her arms tightly around my neck. I tried to put her down on the table, but she continued to scream and wouldn't let go.

After trying for several minutes to take Brittany's vital signs and then trying to examine her without any success, she said, "I've read in Brittany's chart where she had some problems at birth. Her behavior today is a bit worrisome to me. I think we might want to let a pediatric neurologist take a look at her, now that she's older. I don't think this is typical for a two-year old."

Her comment shocked me—it seemed cold, and callous. She'd never seen my daughter before that day and had spent only a few minutes with us now. *How can she already have reached that conclusion?* I thought. *Is it so unthinkable that a child would be upset after a full round of needles?*

I tried to be polite but was angry. I dismissed the whole conversation, and we found a new pediatrician.

Chapter Seven

"YOU NEED TO get out of Mama's garden tub now. You're going to fall and hurt yourself trying to climb."

Brittany ignored me and continued walking in circles around the tub's inner edge, shouting, "Hurt! Like Humpty Dumpty! 'Humpty Dumpty sat on a wall. Humpty Dumpty had a great fall. All the king's horses and all the king's men couldn't put Humpty together again'!"

She repeated this several times. Then, as I put on makeup and held Katelyn in my lap, she recited "The Night Before Christmas" in its entirety. After she finished, she began quoting what was to me a new rhyme.

> Water, water, everywhere,
> And all the boards did shrink;
> Water, water, everywhere,
> Nor any drop to drink.

"Brittany, where did you hear that?"

"Granddaddy told me." (It turned out to be from Coleridge's poem "The Rime of the Ancient Mariner.")

With auburn curls spilling down to her lower back, she looked like a life-sized doll. Not quite three, she could, with exactitude, quote any rhyme or sing any song she'd heard a single time. Her memory was astonishing.

"Mama, I want to see *Pete's Dragon*."

"As soon as I get ready, I'll put the tape in the VCR so you can watch it."

She shot out of the tub and darted to the den. She went to the cabinet where we kept all the videotapes and started scanning the labels. She could name each title in the large collection. She was too young to read, yet by some means of association she could identify every single one.

We found it incredible how she grasped concepts she heard. She laughed in the appropriate places, and she asked incisive questions about the stories. I bought as many educational videos as I could, and she quickly soaked up all the information she could wring from them. She also was fascinated with shows on the Discovery Channel. She simply loved learning.

One night, when we arrived to visit Todd's parents, Brittany hit the ground running.

"Don't go in Grandma's kitchen, Britt—she might be busy right now."

"It's all right, Debbie," Grandma called. "I've got her."

Brittany walked over to the open fridge, and we heard her ask, "How do you know a rat has been in the refrigerator?"

"Hmm—I don't know, Brittany. How *do* you know?"

"Because the cheese is all gone."

Everyone laughed. We assumed she must have heard this on one of her videos. If she heard something one time, she never forgot it.

The girls loved their playroom, and after Katelyn learned to walk, they both were in there every day. Brittany would set the play dishes on the little pink wooden table her grandpa had made, and if Katelyn moved a single item out of place, she'd rush around and move it back into position. Everything had to be in order—*Brittany's* order.

Brittany and Katelyn playing dress up

Further, while she was meticulous when it came to keeping things lined up as she wanted them, there was a twist when it came to her room. She seemed to know exactly where everything belonged—yet to all the rest of us it resembled absolute chaos. You couldn't move an inch in there without stepping on something.

At that stage of our lives, shopping or going out to dinner was a huge challenge. This wasn't because we couldn't handle two small children but rather because Brittany was so unpredictable. She wouldn't sit in a highchair or in someone's lap for any length of time unless something (a book, a song, a movie …) had her undivided attention, thus anything like simple waiting caused issues.

And eating was a challenge of its own. If hungry, Brittany would protest until she got food—she had to have it *that instant*. I finally determined to take crackers everywhere we went. This was something she would not soon outgrow; even as a young teen, hunger would pull her toward something like rage.

When Britt was four, we began noticing a significant difference between the girls' behavior. Katelyn was so laid back, no matter that she now was the one entering the supposed terrible twos; by contrast, we were constantly racing after Brittany, whose boundless energy didn't wane. From the time Katelyn began walking, we could give her a toy, and she'd play with it contently for long periods. Brittany's engine seemed self-fueling as unceasingly she zipped and zapped at full speed from toy to toy and place to place.

She had an insatiable desire to laugh; grabbing something away from Katelyn or doing anything she was asked not to do would send her into hysterics. If she saw me on the phone, she saw a chance to cause mischief. I tried to put markers and scissors and other keep-away items in secret spots, but somehow there was no hiding place in the entire house she eventually wouldn't discover.

My grandmother, who we called "Mamaw," kept both girls during the day while I taught school. I was thrilled that the wonderful woman who'd helped raise me would be helping to raise my children. Mamaw used a strict routine, with ordered daily activities, and routine was important to Brittany—it seemed to help her cope with having to be away from me. When I walked in the door each day after work, Brittany would jump into my arms, bury her face in my hair, and grit her teeth tightly as she hugged me. She would twirl my hair awhile, then she would jump down and begin playing with Katelyn again.

"Debbie, I wonder why she smells your hair like that."

"I don't know, Mamaw. She always does, though, and grits those teeth too."

"I guess it's her way of showing you how much she loves you."

All children have different personalities and develop their own quirks, and Brittany's obsession with my hair had never worried me. The first time I truly became concerned in general with her behavior came one evening as I was cooking dinner. Katelyn was in her highchair, eating, and Brittany was on the floor, playing with her doll.

"Don't run around the table, Brittany. You might get hurt. Don't run around the table, Brittany. You might get hurt. Don't run around the table, Brittany. You might get hurt. Don't run around the table, Brittany. You might get hurt."

I froze. I turned off the burner, and I listened. She repeated this, precisely, dozens and dozens of times, all the while smoothing her doll's hair with her hand. Her eyes were fixed, and she seemed to be staring into space.

I wasn't sure what to think. Those were my exact words she was quoting—I'd said them to her that morning, much earlier in the day. After some minutes had passed, her expression altered, and she looked as if she'd emerged from a trance. Her attention shifted, and she picked up another toy.

A few days later, when I'd just come to think of what had happened as merely a bit peculiar and had finally dismissed it, it happened again.

> "We will go outside when Katelyn wakes up.
> We will go outside when Katelyn wakes up.
> We will go outside when Katelyn wakes up.
> We will go outside when Katelyn wakes up.
> We will go outside when Katelyn wakes up."

Increasingly, then, and almost every day, Brittany was gazing into the distance and parroting back phrases and sentences. This would soon become her norm.

When she started half-day pre-kindergarten, we jokingly cautioned her teacher that she should watch what she said in front of Brittany, as she was like a little recorder that probably would retain and play back statements, questions, exclamations, instructions, and conversations that she'd "captured."

Still, hearing this little girl repeating what she'd heard *was* a wonder. She would reproduce the very intonation and inflection of the person who'd spoken initially. When I'd walk into her room during the evening, she would be repeating phrases and sentences over and over. And it seemed the intensity of her recitals escalated with each day that passed, especially at night.

"You don't need to get into the crayons now, Brittany. We will use them later. You don't need to get into the crayons now, Brittany. We will use them later. You don't need to get into the crayons now, Brittany. We will use them later."

Her repetition seemed to relax her and assist her with winding down from what she had experienced and processed throughout the day. I'd never seen other children do this, and yet it was normal for her, so it became normal to us.

However, during that year we began to see some other things that caused us to give more consideration to her development. Even though she played at home with Katelyn and with cousins who were close to her age, she primarily enjoyed playing alone when at school. She didn't form relationships with any classmates.

We'd been hoping she would begin interacting more with her peers in a more structured setting, but by the end of pre-K she still had no desire to socialize with other children. During free play, she was perfectly content to stay off to the side, alone, instead of joining them on the swings or in a game of chase. It was like she was in a metamorphosis—except that her transformation seemed the opposite of the caterpillar becoming the butterfly. She was gradually leaving the state in which the butterfly flits playfully… and entering back into a cocoon. At night, too, she preferred being alone, in her own little world, playing with her dolls, singing, dancing, and repeating back all manner of "recordings" she'd placed into her memory during the day.

We also began observing that as Katelyn and Brittany grew there was a difference between the ways that they interacted with their cousins. With Katelyn they would pretend to be a family, for instance; they would cook meals on the play stove and rock their dolls together. Brittany never wished to take part. She might be standing nearby, pretending to cook with the pots or pans, but with no desire to enter their pretend world. All her interest remained in her own imaginary realm.

Brittany and Katelyn with their cousins Ashley and Jessica

For age five Brittany had a remarkable vocabulary. Still, she wasn't correlating her abilities into the area of academic performance. After six weeks of kindergarten at the same little school where she'd attended pre-K, we were called in for a conference with her teacher. This would be the first of many emotional meetings we would have with teachers through Brittany's school years.

My nerves were on edge as I drove up to the little gray building with red and blue letters painted on its side. I had known Mrs. Judy a long time; I knew she was very experienced, and I knew she was a straight talker. I was anxious that the little voice in my head, which kept telling me that something wasn't quite right with my little girl, might in some way now have its message confirmed.

After a few minutes of small talk, Mrs. Judy asked me to have a seat. Then, before speaking her first sentence, she was grinning from ear to ear.

"Brittany is a very bright little girl. But you already know that, don't you. I will tell you this: In all my years of teaching kindergarten, I have never met a child quite like her. She learns very quickly, yet there's just something I can't quite put my finger on that's causing me some concern."

"Well, I know her handwriting isn't very good."

"I think her handwriting will get better with time. Right now, that's not at all my focus."

None of what she began to tell me was a surprise. Nevertheless, hearing these words from someone else made them more powerful and painful.

"Brittany seems to be in her own little bubble, not attuned to what's going on around her. Sometimes

I'm not even sure she's aware of her surroundings. While she is progressing academically, I am concerned with her social skills. When everyone else is playing together, taking turns, she's always by herself. I think, if I would let her, she'd spend the whole day collecting acorns under the big oak tree. How would you feel about having her evaluated by our psychologist, to see if there may be an issue we can address?"

My heart felt so heavy. I continued the conference as if I were fine, but afterward I was engulfed in a tide of anxiety. I knew in my heart that Mrs. Judy was right, yet I didn't want to face the fact that my precious child might have a problem.

Night after night I went to bed and prayed that when the school psychologist evaluated Brittany he'd find nothing wrong. I also prayed that she would cooperate during the testing procedure. Anything out of her routine was likely to send her into major unease, so, to prepare her for the visit, I decided to make up a Dugan story.

When she was two or three, I'd begun inventing stories, using a make-believe family, the Dugans, to aid Brittany's adjustment to new routines or interactions she was about to encounter. These helped her understand the "rules" of each situation. For example, before going to a party, I'd place the Dugans in a similar setting.

"Once upon a time there were five Dugans." I'd hold up my hand and wiggle all my fingers. Then I would hold up my thumb and say, "The littlest Dugan didn't always do what his mama asked him to do. When they went to a birthday party, he tried to open the presents even though they weren't his. And do you know what else he did?"

"What did he do, Mama?"

"He ran around and wouldn't sit still while the gifts were opened. He yanked toys away from the other boys and girls, and he pitched a fit when Mama Dugan said it was time to go home."

Brittany would listen, wide-eyed, to every word. "Well, what happened when the littlest Dugan acted that way? What did the Mama Dugan do?"

"You know what would happen, Brittany. What always happened when the littlest Dugan didn't follow the rules?"

She would look at me intently and say, "He went to bed without any supper!"

"You aren't going to act like the littlest Dugan, are you?"

"No ma'am!"

Of course, I never would have sent her to bed without eating, but she seemed to see the bigger picture. What mattered was that she grasped the concept of a right way and a wrong way to act. Sometimes the stories were effective, and sometimes they weren't.

I worked as a teacher in the same school system, so I knew Gordon, the psychologist. When I drove Brittany to school the day of the testing, I described his appearance and explained that he was my friend, to help her feel more comfortable around him.

I sought to illustrate the importance of paying attention and answering "Mr. Gordon's" questions. At the story's conclusion, Brittany said, "I know what happened when the littlest Dugan wouldn't answer the questions, Mama."

"What happened?"

"He went to bed without any supper."

I smiled and took her hand as we walked to her classroom. When she was settled, I walked back to the car, praying that she would cooperate.

Anxious to hear about all that had transpired, I could hardly wait to pick her up that afternoon. Brittany, contrarily, was focused on getting home to watch Mother Goose. In the car, she wouldn't give any information at all, only answering my questions with "yes" or "no" as she stared away and twirled her hair.

Later that week I met with Gordon. After we'd chatted, he pulled a folder from his briefcase and began going over every detail of the testing. He started with results from the Woodcock–Johnson Revised Test of Cognitive Abilities.

"Debbie, Brittany scored within the average range for reading. Her scores for math calculation and broad math were in the low average range."

Both markers staggered me. I was baffled that she hadn't scored higher in reading, knowing her extensive vocabulary and excellent comprehension skills. I also was perplexed about the math levels, as she never seemed to have any trouble with her weekly assignments. I attributed that result to her inattentiveness.

I kept waiting for Gordon to bring up social skills, but he didn't mention this. I certainly wasn't going to ask him. And, in truth, I didn't want to hear anything else.

I felt better afterward, because nothing emerged to

indicate that Brittany was anything but "normal." I guess I was thankful for the ability to stick my head back into the sand for a little while longer.

Brittany playing alone at Kindergarten

The summer following kindergarten, Brittany took a test to see if she would qualify for our city's new Morehouse Magnet School, where I would be teaching. My prayer was that she would focus long enough to take the test (comprised of reading and math), which would determine whether she could attend. We waited several weeks to receive the results, and my nerves were frayed until we received a letter confirming that she'd passed the screening and could enroll.

I didn't know at all how she would handle a full

day of school. After half-day kindergarten she'd always eaten lunch at Mamaw's house. She was a very picky eater and tiny for her age; I was worried about whether she'd eat enough at school. I even worried she wouldn't be able to open the building's doors for lack of upper-body strength.

Her sensitivity to tastes and textures meant she was willing to eat only a few different things, mainly chicken, bread, and potatoes. And she drank milk. But her diet included no vegetables or fruits, no beef or fish, no nuts or beans. I couldn't even get her to eat candy or chew gum!

She wasn't sensitive only to food textures, either—she was just as fastidious about clothing and fabrics. All the tags had to be cut out of her shirts; she only wanted to wear dresses (no pants or shorts) because she didn't like anything fitting tightly around her waist. And she reacted sharply to loud noises; she'd cover her ears every time she flushed the toilet.

Fortunately, Brittany's first grade teacher was structured and organized, so she did well in the classroom and had no problems academically. She still struggled socially, not really making friends with her classmates, but she never seemed to mind. She was content to play alone.

Her teacher always commented that at school Brittany was so quiet, a stark contrast from her behavior at home. And while she was subdued there, she had more energy in the afternoon than when her day began. She climbed; she danced; she ran. Her energy never ebbed from the moment she got home until she fell asleep. It was as though she were a top, wound up slowly throughout the school day, and the moment she re-entered the house all tension released and the spinning began.

Upon finishing first grade Brittany had mastered that level's reading and math skills. Conversely, her handwriting wasn't too legible—It didn't matter how many times we practiced with her letters, the spacing was always wrong and she wrote many of them backwards. I hired a friend, a special education teacher, to see if she could assist Brittany with writing, but after many months of practicing it didn't improve. Katelyn was two years younger, and her handwriting skills had long surpassed Brittany's.

As a teacher of gifted students—those who show high intellectual or artistic capabilities—I was impressed with Brittany's oral language skills and ability to remember what she was taught. At age six she began taking even more interest in reading and would flip through books for hours and hours. While her teacher also said her handwriting would improve with time, I still worried it wouldn't, convinced that she was too intelligent to be unable to understand how to form her letters.

When Brittany entered the second grade she was still struggling to socialize. Her aunt Amy was her teacher, and she tried to help her make friends with her classmates, but Brittany was still interested only in doing what she wanted to do. That didn't include playing with others.

On the brighter side, there was one setting in which she showed a bit of attention to playing with other children: this was in a close-knit group of church friends and family. The group included seven girls, counting Brittany and Katelyn, who became inseparable.

Thus, most of the time, Brittany would appear to remain in a sort of bubble. Thankfully, that bubble was inside another bubble, one that included these other girls close to her age. In time, among many shared activities and adventures, they would attend ballet class together, they would take trips together, they would spend almost every summer weekend swimming or on some other fun outing.

At the same time, when all the other girls spent hours in the pool, Brittany would walk around in the grass, chasing and catching grasshoppers. Occasionally she would join the group... though usually this was to toss a grasshopper or two on them to see how loudly they'd scream. She loved playing practical jokes, and then she would retreat to her solitude.

Life inside our circle of friends seemed ordinary to us, while in reality we were inside the bubble.

Brittany with some of the girls in the bubble (Brittany, Jodi, Meredith, Baylie, Katelyn, Tinsley, and Bradi)

Brittany with her cousins, sister and the girls in the bubble at dance rehersal. **Front row:** Brittany, Meredith, Caroline. **Second row:** Tinsley, Madison, Jodi, Katelyn, and Baylie. **Top:** Bradi

Chapter Eight

As she entered third grade, Brittany continued to write letters backwards and have difficulty with letter spacing. Her challenges with social skills persisted, and her teacher again relayed questions about her inattentiveness during class. There were times she had to be touched on the arm or shoulder to be nudged from the deep trance of her constant thoughts.

We were also concerned that her sensory issues seemed to be intensifying. Loud noises (like fire-drill bells) became almost unbearable to her, and ordinary daily tasks, like brushing her teeth, were unpleasant. She had a high tolerance for pain if, for instance, she fell and scraped her leg or bumped her head, but the simple act of brushing her hair would be an intense battle of wills due to her discomfort with the slight pulling caused by each brushstroke. We decided on a private evaluation by a psychologist to seek more insight. I'd come to realize I could no longer justify leaving this stone unturned.

On the day of the appointment, Brittany first was given the Wechsler Intelligence Scale for Children, a type of IQ test that gauges intellectual abilities and detects learning disabilities. I believed she would score very high—many of the gifted students whom I'd taught had characteristics that I'd likewise seen in her. These included her great fondness for learning, extraordinary reading skill, capacity to memorize virtually anything, comprehension of information and concepts at advanced levels, and ability to express herself verbally well beyond her years.

Therefore, when her evaluation arrived, I couldn't account for why her full-scale score was in the low average range. I didn't see at all how these results could be accurate. Of all things, could *intelligence* truly be the issue here?

The psychologist went on to state that though Brittany had been cooperative, she'd been easily distracted and somewhat anxious throughout the entire test. She'd inquired along the lines of "How much longer?" and "Are there very many more questions?" She'd been restless and had excessive difficulty concentrating.

And then I read: "These scores may be a low estimate of her true cognitive ability." *I knew it!* This couldn't have been a reliable reflection, for whatever other challenges she faced, she was smart—brilliant in many ways.

She also had taken another assessment called the Wechsler Individual Achievement Test… on which she'd been shown to have a significant weakness in comprehension. I literally laughed out loud, then; comprehension was one of her genuine strengths. Straightaway it was obvious that we needed to seek help for her inattention.

Further, "When told that Digit Span was the final subtest, [Brittany] was attentive and did quite well on that subtest." This instantly registered with me too. She had done well because she'd known it was the last ordeal to endure—here she had dug deep and marshaled all her resources.

The report's last section listed the results of the Child Behavior Checklist scales, for diagnosing

ADHD. Based on these, the psychologist determined that Brittany did have attention-deficit/hyperactivity disorder. And, her diagnosis included dysgraphia, a writing disorder. Finally, he recommended that she retake the intelligence test after starting medication for ADHD.

When we'd processed all this information, Todd and I began debating about the medication. Our child was only seven; I thought it might change her personality, and of course we didn't want that at all. On the other hand, without intervention she would fall behind in school. I'd seen this happen many times with students who had ADHD. Their inability to pay attention would cause them to lag in their skills. Already we received repeated notes home, from teachers, stating that she couldn't keep her mind focused during class. She would space out, drifting away to wherever she wanted to be inside her mind and missing the instruction altogether.

Teachers would comment that while Brittany sometimes was "a thousand miles away," her world was full of imagination and creativity. Did socializing *need* to be important to her? Yes, she was quiet at school and in other social situations, but at home she shared frequently, often sounding like a little professor while holding forth about insects, rocks, or other facets of nature. And her humor was magnificent—she consistently had us laughing about one thing or another.

She seemed perfectly content with her life, and at times I felt guilty for trying to alter this.

On the day of Brittany's first Adderall dose, I performed an experiment with her writing. After she'd taken the stimulant, every fifteen minutes I had her sit down and write, "The quick brown fox jumped over the lazy dog," a sentence that contains all twenty-six alphabet characters at least once. I wanted to see if any of her backwards letters improved with the medicine.

After thirty minutes, I saw a noticeable improvement in both her writing and her letter spacing. I even saw her write the letter "b" backwards, then look at it intently, erase it, and write it correctly. After forty-five minutes, her handwriting was markedly more legible. What's more, for the first time in memory, I was amazed to see her walk to her room instead of run.

We were encouraged and agreed to give this medication a try. If she showed side effects, we could always change course. And, after a few weeks of observation, we decided that due to its effectiveness we would continue the Adderall dose.

We were excited about how it aided her. She could stay focused and attentive in the classroom; she began doing well on all assignments. It helped her with impulsivity and hyperactivity too. Before, on a normal day I'd have to call her name at least a hundred times, for she constantly would be climbing on things, taking toys from her cousins and sister, and getting into stuff she wasn't supposed to handle. She was better able to think before she acted, and I didn't have to correct her behavior as much.

The only drawback was how the medicine curbed her appetite. She was already very tiny in size, in the fifth weight percentile for children of her age. Now we worried that she would fall yet further behind, so we made regular visits to her pediatrician, Dr. Dyess, for monitoring her growth.

We didn't tell Brittany at the time about medication for ADHD. We told her that she'd be taking a pill to help her to be calm, to pay attention in class, and to focus. She seemed to be fine with that explanation and didn't question it.

We didn't give her medicine once she got home from school, with the goal that she would eat better at night. However, when she found herself in trouble for climbing on her dresser or running wildly through the house, she'd immediately blame her actions on not having taken her calming pill. So we made sure to let her know that with or without medicine she was responsible for her own behavior.

Brittany continued to grow as a vivacious reader. Still, when writing she always reversed the letters b, c, d, g, j, and s, and numbers such as 3, 5, 6, and 9. Because of this, I wondered if she might have dyslexia (which is primarily related to reading; dysgraphia is mostly related to writing).

To ease my fear, I contacted the Dyslexia Coordinator at the State Department of Education to seek a professional opinion. When I mentioned the backwards letters and numbers, the coordinator told me that at Brittany's age she shouldn't be writing reversals, and that there was a strong possibility she did have dyslexia.

"Let me also say this, then. I'm a teacher and have taught several students with dyslexia, and they always struggled with reading the simplest of words. Brittany doesn't have the slightest trouble reading. In fact, reading is her pastime. She loves it."

"She may not have trouble now, but if she has this many reversals, it's when the reading material gets more difficult that you will see evidence of the dyslexia. I have never seen any child at her age with that many reversals who did not have difficulty with reading, and I've dealt with many children who are dyslexic."

Even after a long conversation, I couldn't convince her that I knew Brittany did not have a reading deficit. We would go in her room at night to find her reading under the covers with a flashlight. She always had a book in her hands.

Accordingly, I began purchasing books about dyslexia and reading everything I could find about it online. I ignored my own instincts, deciding that I needed to learn all I could about the disorder.

My shelves were already lined with books about ADHD, and now there was another row with volume after volume about dyslexia. I must have read every current book out there, and none of them convinced me Brittany was dyslexic, though the state education coordinator had been sure she knew otherwise. I was certain that handwriting, not reading, was the issue.

After no luck with exhaustive searches to uncover an exact match for Brittany's characteristics, I determined that instead of trying to find a diagnosis I'd focus my attention on her strengths and find ways around her writing disability. One night, surfing the Internet for ideas and means that might be of benefit,

I found an advertisement for a small handheld computer called an AlphaSmart.

"Todd, look at this." I turned my laptop around so he could see. "If I can teach Brittany how to type on this little computer, she can do all of her writing on it. The reviews agree that it's very durable."

He took the laptop and began reading the ad. "This might work. But do you think she's old enough to type?"

"I think there's no reason we can't try it. The keyboard is smaller than usual—looks like her fingers would fit on the keys. If it works, great. If not, well, at least we gave it a shot."

From the moment it arrived, Brittany loved her mini handheld and eagerly started pecking out her spelling words, homework, and other written assignments. She began expressing herself more, and she wrote creatively. Up until then, her stories usually had been short and to the point. When she used her AlphaSmart she commenced to fashion lengthy stories and poems and reports, several of which won school writing contests.

While the Adderall and the AlphaSmart weren't end-all cures, they absolutely gave Brittany a hand in coping with everyday tasks. When she took the medication, she and Katelyn would interact more when they played together. Then Katelyn began to pass Brittany in height and weight, and because she always acted like an older sister, most people thought that she was.

Katelyn's birthday is in late December, and as the girls got older, we were more certain than ever that God had sent us a most special Christmas gift when He'd given us our second child. She had motherly instincts toward Brittany, and she was patient even when Brittany didn't share or wouldn't wait her turn while playing a game or always had to have her way when deciding what they would play. When Brittany would close herself off and remain ensconced in her own reality, it was Katelyn who would draw her out as much as possible.

Every year we saw the gap widen between Brittany's social behavior and the development of Katelyn and the other girls within the bubble. They were all enrolled in dance together, and while Brittany loved to dance, she struggled to tear away from her train of thoughts to listen to the instructor and follow the steps with the others. At home she would put on her ballet shoes and dance for us with real poise, and yet adhering to directions and remaining connected in class was difficult; her mind took her elsewhere.

Despite the ADHD medication, social inattentiveness was still a substantial factor. Her focus on a TV show would be so all-encompassing that I'd have to turn off the screen before she could process that I was in the room. Even after her pediatrician increased the dosage, more than periodically she would zone out.

"Brittany, Dr. Dyess said that she wants you to visit a new doctor—he can tell us if there is a better medicine for helping you concentrate on your schoolwork."

"Who is the new doctor, Mama?"

"His name is Dr. Brown."

"Do I have to take a test?"

For her, a test represented pure torture, because it meant she had to stay focused for a lengthy period. I hated to put her through more of this, but Dr. Dyess's opinion was that at this stage additional examination and diagnosis could be crucial. Brittany was nine now, and it seemed that year by year her social struggles had become more and more significant.

The clinic was a couple of hours from home, so we decided to make it a fun trip too. After the drive we spent the night at a hotel and took the girls swimming.

They enjoyed the pool, and before bed I tried to prepare Brittany for her appointment the next day. I told her a Dugan story to familiarize her with how the specialists would ask questions. When the girls finally fell asleep, I stared at their beautiful faces and then closed my eyes, praying that God would reveal what we needed to understand about how to help our daughter.

"Lord, please give us strength to confront the evaluation's outcome head on. I know you love us, and I know you had a plan for Brittany's life even before she was born. Help me to accept that plan, whatever it might be."

For some reason I instinctively knew that this time the testing would reveal more than I wanted to hear. I also knew that Brittany had many layers of uniqueness, and I truly wanted to recognize and appreciate each one.

When we woke the next morning and began readying to go to the psychologist's office, Todd leaned over and kissed Katelyn and Brittany on their foreheads.

"How did that bed sleep last night, girls?"

Katelyn rubbed her eyes and mumbled, "Fine, Daddy."

Brittany looked at him very seriously and said, "Beds don't sleep, Daddy."

Katelyn started laughing. "Not the *bed*, Brittany."

Brittany took everything we said literally, and her words that morning gave me a perfect example to share with the specialists. No matter how much she enjoyed language, figurative speech was difficult for her to grasp.

Todd and Katelyn dropped us off in front of the clinic and then went back to the hotel until we were done. When we walked through the doors and sat down in the waiting room, we were surrounded by pamphlets on tables and bookshelves. I picked up several on ADHD and found that they all described Brittany. She wasn't as hyperactive as she'd been as a small child, but she was more withdrawn now, daydreaming more than she was living in the real world.

I met with the doctor first, while Brittany remained with his assistant. I answered many of his questions. After he had perused the information that we'd written out to describe and exemplify our concerns, he asked about attention span, handwriting issues, and interaction with others.

He then asked if I thought Brittany expressed emotion "in a normal manner." I said that though she kept her feelings hidden deep within, they were there—I had seen them. I said that even at age four she'd seemed to have a profound awareness of the pain of others. I told him how, for instance, she had stood before the TV when a commercial for feeding the hungry had aired, and how, when she saw the children, their stomachs swollen from starvation, a single tear had rolled down her cheek. Clearly, she understood and experienced complex emotions, and thus I didn't see how she could display so little understanding of common, ordinary do's and don'ts relating to social interactions.

I'd gotten a glimpse of the emotions she felt upon the loss of my father, who died from cancer. She had been very close to him; they'd read nursery rhymes together, caught lizards and bugs together, and loved to discuss shared interests in history and science. When I told her he'd passed away, she had shed tears, wiped them off her cheeks, and said, "He's in heaven now, isn't he?" Then, like a switch in her mind had been flipped, she set aside her feelings and went back to playing with her favorite toy. For that brief instant I'd seen how she experienced grief. I was sure her feelings really were there all the time, and I wanted to find out how that switch was turned on and off, no matter how well hidden it was from all of us.

I told of how Brittany became fixated on different topics in her books. When she had read about the life of Harriet Tubman, I'd found her sitting in the middle of her bedroom floor, looking sad. She'd marked all over her new white shirt with a black pen to make it look dirty. She told me she wanted to make herself look like Harriet, the slave, and that she secretly thought about how she might have helped Harriet if she too had lived during that time.

I described how she took everything that was said literally, and about when she told my mother that what she really needed was to buy a Sprint phone, because that way she could get some common sense "for free." That's what Sprint's ad had promised. When I asked if she really believed the company was doling out common sense, she looked at me and replied, without hesitating, "That's what they said."

I also recounted the conversation from that very morning, with her daddy, about beds sleeping.

When the psychologist asked if Brittany liked routine, I laughed. "That's an understatement." I told the story of Todd having been away a few weeks, working, and then deciding to surprise her by picking her up from school an hour earlier than the regular dismissal time. Brittany had cried—she didn't want to leave with him because that wasn't the time she was supposed to be picked up from school.

And I explained that she seemed to have no fear, and so we had to watch her constantly. She would climb on top of my car, anywhere, to sit on the roof, or she would walk across busy lots without ever looking for vehicles. I mentioned that she sometimes seemed anxious even with no reason to worry, and that in this mode she would twirl her hair, pull at her collar, and repeatedly clear her throat.

By now I was feeling as though everything I was describing was so *negative*. I desperately wanted the doctor to understand Brittany's uniqueness. "She's extremely creative. When she plays dress-up, she can design a costume out of anything! She's wonderfully inventive, when she stops reading long enough to engage with her sister and cousins."

I also went through the long process of detailing her letter reversals and attention struggles, describing how, despite medication, she still dealt with inattentiveness and didn't really communicate with anyone but family unless she was asked a question. I ended the interview by saying how much she enjoyed sitting in her room, echoing phrases from the day, playing with her rock collection, or cutting up tiny pieces of paper that covered her floor—when she did this it looked like a post-parade scene, where streets are littered with brightly colored confetti.

Afterward he asked if he could talk with Brittany alone. Then, following what seemed like hours, he opened the door and brought her back out to the lobby. Finally, he met again with me and pledged that when he'd gone back over all his notes he would write up his report and have it ready to send to us within a few days.

Waiting for those results was very difficult. As I read my Bible each night, I was comforted by verses like Isaiah 41:10:

> Do not fear, for I am with you;
> do not be dismayed, for I am your God.
> I will strengthen you and help you;
> I will uphold you with my righteous right hand. (NIV)

God's Word reminded me that no matter what the doctors said, He would be with us, and He would be with Brittany too.

When we finally received the letter from the psychologist and psychiatrist, I opened it and quickly scanned the pages. Part of their diagnosis was the same as the previous findings of ADHD and dysgraphia—but there also was a new one this time. Listed under attention-deficit/hyperactivity disorder and dysgraphia were the words "pervasive developmental disorder."

I had taught school for many years. I'd seen many students who suffered with ADHD and a few with dyslexia. But I had never *heard* of pervasive developmental disorder.

I stood motionless with my eyes fixed on those three words. I had no idea what they meant. I quickly found my laptop and entered the term into the Google search bar. The first thing that popped up on the screen was a box containing a definition. My heart sank when I read it. Pervasive developmental disorder meant autism.

Chapter Nine

After the initial shock of learning that Brittany was on the autism spectrum, once again we were determined to do everything we could to get her the help she needed to reach her full potential. Todd and I decided not to tell anyone else about her diagnosis until it became necessary. I had seen students who'd been labeled and put in special education classes fall through the cracks in school. I knew from experience that sometimes children were treated differently when given a label. I was resolute that she would not become a victim to this.

Moreover, from that day forward I was devoted to becoming as knowledgeable as possible about autism.

According to the National Institutes of Health, "autism is known as a 'spectrum' disorder because there is wide variation in the type and severity of symptoms [that] people experience." Within the past decade, three conditions that previously had been classified separately—autistic disorder, Asperger's syndrome, and, Brittany's diagnosis, pervasive developmental disorder non-specified—have been combined into one diagnosis: autism spectrum disorder. After reading several more books I also was convinced that she displayed some of the characteristics of Asperger's.

At the same time, I redoubled my efforts to be just as focused on Brittany's many strengths. She had almost perfect pitch; she savored music and poured over books; she loved science and history. Her memory was phenomenal, and while her handwriting was still almost illegible, she was blessed with the ability to write poetry and stories. She celebrated life and frequently was laughing, telling jokes, and singing when at home or around her cousins and the girls in the bubble. She and Katelyn spent many evenings giving us concerts featuring songs they'd learned at church or from videos. We were granted the privilege of seeing this wonderful side of her on a regular basis, even if around other people she would retreat into a quiet solitude.

While striving to avoid having her labeled, we

knew now too that Brittany would require an individualized education plan so she could get the necessary in-school therapy to work on delays in writing and social skills. She needed some accommodations and modifications, like shortened assignments and use of a computer for written projects. The school also would do their own evaluation before developing her plan.

This was the first time Brittany would take an IQ test while on medication for ADHD. Another exam would measure her math and reading abilities. I was anxious to see what these assessments would reveal.

When I was called into the meeting with the teachers, the diagnostician, and the school psychologist to discuss results, I feared hearing about a new diagnosis—yet another type of disorder that would send me back online for still more research. I was dealing with a sense of overwhelm and a dread that either the end of discoveries was unreachable or that we might run into a diagnosis worse than anything previous. Instead I was told that Brittany's reading ability was above a sixth-grade level, and her math abilities were within the high average range. Her IQ results were amazing.

She did receive another diagnosis that day: this

time it was "gifted." She would be moved from regular classes to a type of resource class in which she'd receive specialized instruction in the areas of her strengths. *Finally,* we had confirmation of what I'd believed since she was a toddler: Brittany was no ordinary child. Yes, there were substantial difficulties and trials ahead of her, but she likewise had talents that would help her to surmount whatever she needed to face.

Brittany around the time of her diagnosis of "gifted"

In relatively short order, Brittany's accommodations were in place. The teacher for her gifted class, Mrs. Richard, truly seemed to understand her needs, a huge blessing. And our daughter began to thrive in school. Up until then, each year I would have been interacting with each teacher, sharing some of Brittany's social difficulties and relaying some of her talents and other aspects of her personality. I had always been afraid they would take a look at her handwriting and make a false assumption about her intelligence.

Now she genuinely flourished. Within the class's small setting she opened up more. She began expressing her feelings there. She started being willing to speak about the literature they studied. More and more of what was inside her began to be more and more visible to others.

She read novels in class and pondered her insights on their themes. We decided she'd already outgrown her AlphaSmart, so we purchased a laptop for her to use at school. Even so, we had to encourage her to use it because she began to enjoy writing with pencil and paper! Her handwriting had not noticeably improved, yet she filled journal after journal with original poetry and stories that revealed much deeper insight into her thoughts.

She received physical therapy a few days a week at school, and we also decided to bring her to a private occupational therapist for yet more aid with fine motor skills, balance, and coordination. God put into our path Melissa, a therapist who immediately made a special connection with Brittany and became determined to help her overcome some of her struggles. Melissa sometimes would involve Katelyn to bring out the Brittany we saw at home, so active and vital, instead of the Brittany others saw in most social settings, quiet and withdrawn. We drove the forty miles roundtrip three days every week and never failed to see progress.

I enrolled both girls in piano classes too, so between school and dance and all the rest our weeks were full. The girls loved to sing; I wanted them to have a good background in music. I'd grown up playing three different instruments and shared this passion with them. Katelyn caught on to the lessons faster than Brittany, but I was pleased to see Brittany stick with it, though it was very difficult for her.

Brittany never knew of our behind-the-scenes work to ensure she was able to get the needed educational accommodations. By this point, and even before, she wouldn't have been able to function in school without a laptop; in the elementary grades she already had needed modifications like shortened assignments and oral testing. Each year it had become more and more difficult to show her teachers she was bright: she'd never answered questions in class, to share her knowledge. Instructors seeing her handwriting had seen, at best, a kindergartener's learning level. I always brought a copy of a poem, in her own handwriting, and that same poem typed out, to better illustrate the depth and scope of her thought processes.

It didn't catch me off guard that some teachers didn't want to follow her individualized education plan. As a teacher, I myself had sometimes offered some of the same excuses for resisting accommodations and modifications. *I'd* been the one who asked, "If we give students these crutches during their school years, aren't we setting them up for failure when they get out of school?"

When Brittany's disabilities were diagnosed, I finally realized that it's not a teacher's job to worry about how students with disabilities will cope with life after the classroom. My task as a teacher is to make sure every child is able to learn while she or he is in the classroom.

(A poem Brittany wrote in her fourth-grade gifted class)

"Courage"

We're all gallant and strong
Like the bang of an old gong
In our hearts a fiery seed
This key that we possess
Can be wakened from its rest
Can be used to make our courage run free
Courage is fiery gold
That our hearts can soon behold
If only we would choose to set it free

"Imagination's Beauty"

Imagination takes its flight
Riding on an eagle's wings
Beholding quite a different sight
Of Maidens fair and fairy wings

Elves dancing in the dale
Beneath the setting sun
Witches casting magic spells
Adventures just begun

Close your eyes or read a book
If only you could see
Magic exists if you only look
Imagination is the key
(Another fourth-grade poem of Brittany's)

A couple of years later, when Brittany was almost thirteen and in seventh grade, we were at a checkup with Dr. Dyess. During routine measurements, she found that Brittany's height ratio to her peers had dropped significantly, and she suggested we go to an endocrinologist to determine whether she was confronting a growth problem. She'd been small for her age from the start, and we'd always assumed it was her eating habits that kept her from gaining weight and being taller. Now it seemed there might be a different reason.

"Dr. Dyess, do you think the medicine she's taking for ADHD could be stunting her growth?"

"I don't think that's it. For years she was around the fifth percentile in height and weight, and that didn't change when she started the medication *or* during the rest of the time that she has taken it. Now, though, she's markedly below that ratio."

Dr. Dyess made a recommendation for us, and within a few weeks we drove to New Orleans to consult with the endocrinologist. When we met with Dr. Rao, we learned that our pediatrician's suspicions were correct. Brittany did have a growth disorder, and she would need to begin daily injections of human growth hormone.

At the end of our visit, Dr. Rao's assistant took out a HumatroPen, which looked something like a regular writing pen but with a needle in it. She began using it on an orange to demonstrate how we would inject Brittany's leg. Suddenly, keeping my composure was very difficult. I tried to hold it together as we took turns practicing, giving the shot by poking the orange.

When we returned to the hotel, I went into the

bathroom so the girls and Todd wouldn't see me. I wept, and I prayed. "God, why does she have to suffer this? I can't *imagine* her being stuck by a needle every single day. She has endured so many trials in her short time on this earth. Why can't she have a normal life?"

Thankfully I realized right away my prayer was a selfish one. In that moment I felt guilty for asking such silly questions. God had continually blessed us, in more ways than we could count, and I considered the many dimensions of Brittany's unique personality. The miraculous wonder that was our daughter was immeasurably better than any so-called "normal."

Todd knew I would be hard-pressed to handle giving the shots, but when he had to be out of town for work this would be my responsibility. Katelyn was always there, trying to distract Brittany so she wouldn't focus on the pain. And Brittany managed it better than I ever did. She constantly reminded me, "No pain, no gain, Mama!"

We measured her height weekly, and over several months we began to see some growth! We all agreed that in light of their effect the shots were worth it.

Not too long after this growth spurt, we were at the pediatrician's office again. When Brittany hopped off the examining table and bent down to tie her shoe,

Dr. Dyess said, "Brittany, come stand in front of me for a minute."

She had Brittany bend down, and I noticed she was looking at her back.

"Debbie, I think Brittany may have some curvature in her spine."

I came nearer to look, and there it was. Her spine certainly looked like it was curving to the right.

"I think we need to make an appointment for you with my friend Dr. King. He's an orthopedic surgeon in New Orleans."

"Do you think she has scoliosis?"

"For now, what I can say is that there is unquestionably some curvature."

Later, before I made the call to Todd—which I was dreading—I sat alone, staring blankly. Just that month our pastor had preached about how, in one way or another, we're always entering one of three phases in life: either entering a storm, going through a storm, or coming out of a storm. I felt like our family was in a hurricane that had stalled right over us. And it seemed we were forever entering a phase that presented another different medical diagnosis.

I looked up the passage he had quoted from the psalmist:

> We live within the shadow of the Almighty, sheltered by the God who is above all gods. This I declare, that he alone is my refuge, my place of safety; he is my God, and I am trusting him. For he rescues you from every trap and protects you.... He will shield you with his wings!... His faithful promises are your armor. Now you don't need to be afraid of the dark anymore, nor fear the dangers of the day; nor dread the plagues of darkness, nor disasters in the morning. (Psalm 91:1–6 tlb)

These promises gave me comfort as I began to dial Todd's phone.

We spent the following few days making appointments and reservations for our next trip. We'd been to Children's Hospital New Orleans before, including a visit for testing to determine if Brittany had celiac disease. And we'd been elated then that the results had come back negative—a positive would have meant that some of the few things she did eat would have been off limits to her.

The day we arrived, I could tell Brittany was very anxious, and yet she seemed to recognize the importance of the visit. She sat quietly and twisted her hair until a nurse called her back for X-rays. Then we were led to a room to wait, and within a few minutes a man in a white lab coat entered, holding a folder. Dr. Andrew King put us both at ease very quickly with his kind demeanor and smile. He spoke with a heavy Australian accent, and Brittany seemed to hang on each word. After placing the films under the light, he welcomed her over for a look. He pointed out the curve in her spine, using his pen to demonstrate where her alignment wasn't straight. When he'd completed a brief examination, he spoke directly to me.

"Now, Mom, what we want to do is keep this curvature from increasing. If we can't, we would need to operate and use rods to straighten Brittany's spine with the intent of preventing complications it might cause as she gets older." He went on to explain the possibility that a brace around her torso, to be worn throughout each night, could either slow down or even stop further curvature.

When I saw the model of the hard-plastic brace that would fit tightly under her arms, down to her waist, my heart sank. I couldn't fathom Brittany wearing it, ever. How would we work around her sensory issues to persuade her to sleep in this device *every night*?

She was older now, almost thirteen, and reasoning with her was much easier. She had outgrown Dugan stories years earlier, and I knew she would understand why this was needed. Nonetheless I was afraid I would not be able to convince her.

After we returned home, we had a separate appointment where she was fitted for the brace. Within a few weeks we got the call that it was ready, and when we picked it up, Katelyn came along with us.

"Look, Brittany. It's pink, just like you wanted."

Brittany tried it on and even seemed proud of it. That night I found a thin shirt for her to put on underneath, so it wouldn't be right up against her skin. Then Todd fastened the four Velcro strips around her.

"That's too tight, Daddy."

He loosened them, very slightly. We were grateful that she only had to wear the brace at night. Yet I knew that getting her to keep it on, the whole night, would be no easy task.

Todd re-tightened the Velcro, Brittany climbed into bed, and we turned out the lights.

That first night seemed never to end. I realized then, all over again, how strong-willed my child was and how much determination she had. Whenever we thought she'd fallen asleep, once more we would hear the Velcro opening and know that she was loosening the straps.

Finally, I said, "Todd, I'm going to have to go in and sleep in her bed."

"I guess you will. This isn't going to be easy."

After more hours through which both Brittany and I had shed many tears, she relented. Every night thereafter became just a little easier for her. And, eventually, wearing the brace would become routine.

Chapter Ten

As eighth grade ended for Brittany, I began focusing on the upcoming year. Since the Magnet School went only through junior high, she now would transfer to the high school. She was just 4'8" in height, she weighed under ninety pounds, and for the first time she'd be on a campus without either her sister or me.

She would also be without her resource teachers, including Sandy, one of my best friends, who had helped advocate for her accommodations and modifications throughout her elementary and junior high years. Brittany had been placed in Sandy's hearing-impaired resource room for an hour a day after she was diagnosed with a high frequency hearing loss.

This led to some anxiety for us all, yet we were so fortunate that one of our best friends, Jami, who'd already worked for years with Brittany, daily, would be moving there too.

"Mama, is Ms. Jami going to help me get to my classes?"

"Yes, I'm sure she will help you with your schedule, and remember, you will be able to leave your class five minutes before the bell rings so you can get to your next room before the hallways are crowded. And you'll be allowed to ride the elevator, and to use a rolling backpack so you won't hurt your back."

"I want to stay at the Magnet School. I'm going to miss Mrs. Richard."

"Mrs. Tappin will be your new teacher for gifted, and I know her. She's very nice. You're going to like her. Have you prayed about it?"

"Not really."

"Do you think that would be a good idea?"

Brittany had grown up in church and from girlhood had loved hearing stories from the Bible. Though usually she didn't seem to be paying attention to Sunday school lessons, the teacher could ask her anything and she would know the answer. At a very early age she comprehended what Jesus had done for her on the cross, and she had accepted Him as Lord of her life as a younger teen. After this, much of her writing had begun to focus on Him, on her relationship with Him, and on her understanding of the depth of His love for her.

"I know God will take care of me. I'm just a little scared."

⁓

As the year began, Brittany adjusted better than I could have dreamed. While she'd long been accustomed to a tight educational structure, it turned out she was ready for some academic freedom, and high school gave this to her. She got to choose personal-interest elective courses, like theatre. She loved her English class and the reading that came along with it.

She was getting along beyond any of our hopes. It was then that we found out her spine's curvature had worsened drastically over the summer. Doctors said our only course of action was fusion surgery, and that the procedure wouldn't wait.

We spent another night in New Orleans, awaiting the early morning operation. Before bed, Brittany was very anxious about undergoing general anesthesia and about the surgery itself. She'd been silent for a time when I saw a little grin appear on her face.

"Mama, if I accidentally drank some water after midnight, I wouldn't be able to do the surgery, would I?"

"No, you wouldn't. But then we would have to stay another night and you'd have the operation the next day. Do you need to hear a Dugan story?"

"Mama!"

I laughed, but then I don't think I slept a wink, concerned about whether she *would* get out of bed and drink water to try escaping the hospital. Apparently, she accepted that one way or another she couldn't avoid the ordeal, and she didn't attempt any countermeasures.

The next morning the waiting room was full. We ended up standing against a wall in front of the nurses' station, listening for our name to be called. I was feeling we were completely alone in the crowd when God quickly showed me that He was right there with us and that we would walk through the looming valley together.

An elevator door opened, and we were surprised to see four men from church. "Well, hello, Todd," Brother Cal said as he extended his hand to shake. While Todd spoke with them, I noticed that a nurse at the reception desk kept looking our way. After a few minutes she motioned for me to come to the desk.

"I'm sorry. Are we being too loud?"

"Not at all. I was wondering if you've heard about our Angel Plan?"

"Angel Plan—no, I haven't."

"It's designed to help parents cover the remaining balance once insurance has paid its part. Here, you can fill out these papers, and I'll make sure they get into the right hands."

Paying for doctors and therapists had always taken a toll on our finances. Through this smiling woman's thoughtfulness, and through the sacrificial kindness of those who'd traveled for hours to be with us, I knew the Lord was there with us also. He was taking care of our financial needs as well as encouraging and strengthening us through our pastor and friends.

As Brittany was prepped and wheeled away, we were brought to a small room to stay until the operation was finished. While we waited, I felt the same knot in my stomach that I'd had on our drive to the neonatal unit when she was a baby, so many years earlier. When we prayed, however, a calmness washed over me. This too was the very serenity with which God had blessed me many, many times when I'd felt powerless and afraid.

After five hours in surgery, Dr. King entered.

"Mr. and Mrs. Wilson, Brittany did fine. We didn't encounter anything unexpected, and we're confident that the rods will correct the curvature. She does have some swelling—that's entirely normal. For now, she will be in recovery another hour, and then we'll move her, to her own room. You can follow the nurse there and wait until she's brought in. Okay? And I'll be back to check on her in the morning."

When they wheeled in Brittany, she was hooked up to machines, and I almost gasped when I saw her face, swollen to twice its regular size. I watched tears welling in Katelyn's eyes as Todd hugged her gently. She was fiercely protective of her beloved big sister.

"She's going to be fine, Katie. Dr. King said the swelling is routine, remember? It'll go down in a day or two."

Each day the nurses would help Brittany into a chair, to sit for an hour. Then she would walk the hallway, up and back, up and back, up and back, slowly, tiny step by tiny step, building her strength. When she'd been in the hospital close to a week, we were better able to apprehend the long recuperation ahead: Dr. King firmly recommended that she not return to school for the entirety of the semester.

Katelyn and Brittany as we were leaving the hospital

Following this protocol would require a homebound educator. And God once again took care of Brittany's needs. The school allowed Jami, her resource teacher and our close family friend, to come to our house every weekday and assist her in keeping up with her lessons.

The aim had been for a midyear return to the school campus. This didn't go quite as we'd planned. Shortly before her scheduled resumption of regular classes, Brittany began complaining off and on about dizzy spells. One evening, when I walked into her room, she was sitting on the floor and didn't look right.

"What's wrong, Britt?"

"I'm dizzy again."

I checked her pulse. "Have you been up to anything? Your heart is racing."

"Only reading my book."

When I called Dr. Dyess's office and described her symptoms, the nurse was concerned and instructed us to go to the emergency room. Doctors admitted Brittany, yet after monitoring her vital signs and running tests they couldn't ascertain a cause. Her heartbeat remained rapid for several days, and her cardiologist, Dr. Terry King, decided she would need to begin taking medication to regulate it.

The prescribed medicine initially worked well, but within a few weeks we observed side effects. One day, while she was reading on the couch with her bare feet on the coffee table, I glanced over and was startled.

"Brittany, what's wrong with your feet?"

"Nothing, why?"

"Something isn't right—look at your toes."

She saw, as I had, that all ten of them were a dark purple color.

"Are they cold?"

"I don't think so."

I placed my hands on her toes; they felt like ice. The next day we went to Monroe to see her cardiologist again. This time the diagnosis was Raynaud's Syndrome, a rare disease that causes narrowing of the blood vessels and thus poor circulation. Starting out, the two biggest precautions were that she'd need to wear warm socks and avoid being outside during cold weather.

Katelyn and Brittany during their high school years

As we departed, I saw that Brittany was smiling and shaking her head.

"What's funny?"

"I think you should rename me."

"What do you mean by that?"

"You may as well call me 'Syndrome Queen.'"

We laughed as we drove away. Her sense of humor was even more special during the hard times.

Brittany encountered another wrinkle now too: Her cardiologist determined that she shouldn't return to school until the heart-medication dose was sufficiently adjusted to keep her heartbeat regular. The result was that she would end up spending her freshman year doing all work from home. We got used to stacks and stacks of textbooks on the dining table; her head was buried in books day and night. When she got focused, she would read at all hours, for hours and hours.

She needed opportunities to share and interact with others, though, so she wouldn't slip back into isolation. During that span, one way I facilitated this was by endeavoring to plan a time each night when we would talk together about everyone's day. Each of us would ask a question to help get our conversation going.

Once, when Brittany was about to ask a question, she looked at me. She paused for a good while, staring, and then at last she said, "Mama, would you tell me about Aunt Kathy?"

I was stunned. Wondering what had triggered the topic, I replied, "Well... Kathy was beautiful, and talented, and she loved being around people. Why do you ask?"

"That's not what I want to know."

"What do you want to know?"

"Why did she die?"

When the girls were younger and had seen pictures of my sister, they sometimes would ask about her. I had told them that she'd been killed and that it had been a very sad time for our family. They'd never really inquired further, and as I did not enjoy talking about it the matter rarely was brought up in any context.

Now, Brittany began digging in, forming one query after another. I was flustered and growing frustrated too, yet because she couldn't read my body language to see that I was getting emotional, she kept firing off questions about Kathy's death. I didn't want to open up. "Don't you remember? I've already told you about this before."

"Where was she when she was killed?"

"She was close to the college."

"How did they kill her?"

"It's hard to—"

"Was she kidnapped?"

"Well, … "

"Why would somebody want to hurt her, Mama?"

"Britt, to tell you the truth, I don't really *know* what happened to Kathy!"

"Why don't you know? Don't you want to know? She's your sister. If something ever happened to Katelyn, I would want to know what happened."

Katelyn saw that my eyes had filled with tears. In contrast to Brittany's challenges in reading expressions or perceiving the feelings of others, she was highly intuitive when it came to observing and discerning emotions.

"Brittany, you don't need to ask Mama all these questions. You're making her feel sad."

Brittany never intentionally hurt others, and I knew she hadn't meant to hurt me. Sometimes she said things that weren't appropriate in certain social settings because she lacked the take-others'-emotions-into-account filter that most people have. When she was little, I'd told a lot of Dugan stories to illustrate how words can affect others.

Our conversation about my sister was pulling up emotions I'd suppressed for well over two decades. And this would get me not only to feeling, but also to thinking.

"You are absolutely right, Brittany. I should want to know what happened to Kathy."

That night I went to bed knowing it was true. Why hadn't I ever tried to learn more about my sister's death? Brittany's inquiries would remain with me for quite some time.

Ultimately, I commenced a journey on a long road that would lead to answers to all those questions and more. Through the process, life would come full circle as once more I would meet and then become friends with Dorothy, the woman who fifteen years earlier had encouraged us in the neonatal unit—and who was sister to one of the other girls who in a short span of time had been murdered in our area.

Brittany's sophomore, junior, and senior years were the most pleasant of her entire school career. She had Katelyn and her closest friends there with her, and Mrs. Tappin, teacher for her gifted class, discovered the love for drama that we'd seen when a younger Brittany had performed scenes from films like *Annie* or when the sisters and cousins had acted out their own commercials and stories. Mrs. Tappin encouraged her to participate in school productions, and we even persuaded her to join a local theatre group where she received speaking parts in several youth plays. It was a thrill and a delight to watch her take the stage at The Rose Theatre and play a role.

All the time we'd invested in bringing Brittany for occupational therapy with Melissa was paying off. The myriad hours they'd spent in role-playing dialogues, designed to show how to start conversations and express feelings with others, seemed to be taking hold. Brittany was gaining ground socially; interacting with others was becoming almost second nature to her! Seeing how she matured during that time period was inexpressibly marvelous.

Acting gave her confidence. In her senior year she began to seek out other students who, like her, didn't quite fit in with the popular crowd. She offered encouragement to them by complimenting their strengths and by sharing her own story.

Then, just when all these things were going well, I received my own diagnosis, of kidney cancer. This would be a traumatic season in our lives, and for Brittany, though it was frightening, it also would be one of great character growth. For so long I had been her outlet, her means of expressing herself, and now she was confronted with the fear of losing me.

"Girls, Mama went to the doctor today."

Brittany sat down slowly beside her daddy on the couch. "What did he say?"

"He told us that Mama has kidney cancer."

Katelyn and Brittany both fell into my arms and cried.

"Are you going to die, Mama?"

In our family the word *cancer* had been like a death sentence—we'd lost my grandmother and my daddy within a two-year span to the disease. But that night, no matter that she'd been given this crushing news, Brittany wrote in her diary that for some reason she had peace that everything was going to be okay if she trusted in the Lord. She thanked Him for granting her the peace that put a song in her heart and a smile on her face.

Her maturity during that struggle was inspiring. She even wrote a letter for me to take when I went to Texas for surgery.

> Dear Mama,
>
> I continually think about you. I love you so much. I know God has made you strong. Wherever you are, whatever you go through, don't ever fret because God carries you. Your dad would be very proud of your strength right now.
>
> Love,
> Brittany

I couldn't help but contemplate how, yet again, *she* was the one showing the strength.

After scrutinizing the scans and bloodwork taken there, my oncologist at MD Anderson Cancer Center in Houston reached the same diagnostic conclusion. He planned to remove my adrenal gland and an entire kidney. Surgery followed a few days later.

I had prayed that the cancer would be contained. And when the post-op pathology report came back, we were amazed to find that God had healed me in a way of which I could not have imagined. The specialist was speechless: the report showed no cancer. The updated diagnosis was renal oncocytoma, a rare condition usually found in older men. Its benign tumors are almost always asymptomatic, yet I had evidentiary signs of cancer: weight loss, pain, and loss of appetite.

Radiologists normally can distinguish renal oncocytoma from renal cancer because of the presence of a central scar on the tumor. My scans revealed no such scar. Growths of this type are so rare in the adrenal gland that the literature contains fewer than thirty reported cases. The odds of having that type of tumor in both the adrenal gland and a kidney resemble those of winning the national lottery twice.

Not only was I healed of my disease, I also was

comforted to realize that even if I'd succumbed, our daughter *knew* that her courage and fortitude didn't come from her mama. They came from the Lord.

We saw many other ways Brittany matured during that year. She began singing in a group at church and being assertive during classes. While her interest in boys hadn't ever been delayed, she'd been so shy and introverted that she hadn't yet dated or had a boyfriend. When she began participating in the theatre, this changed. She began talking with one of the guys in the play and developed her first real friendship with a boy.

Later, in chemistry class she met a bright young man with whom she shared many interests. They would talk for hours and seemed truly to enjoy each other's company; he became one of her good friends and asked her to their senior prom. That became her first date.

Throughout high school Brittany had excelled academically, and when her name was called at Class Night (baccalaureate) to announce that she had received full scholarships to two local universities, Todd and I beamed with pride. This was the child who wasn't supposed to be able to read—the child who couldn't write a legible sentence!

Yes, she was disabled, but she was *able* as well—she was able to overcome all the obstacles that her disabilities caused her to confront. In addition to all the unquantifiable rewards, the years of concentrating on her strengths instead of her weaknesses had paid off scholastically. She graduated sixth in her class.

Brittany dressed for prom

Chapter Eleven

"Mama, do you really think I can go to college? You know my visual perception problems affect more than my handwriting—and since I can't drive, how would I even get to and from Monroe? It's almost twenty-five miles away. And it's such a big school. And Katelyn won't be there."

"Brittany, your Aunt Kim works at the university—she will bring you, each day. And that means anytime you have a need, she'll be right there on campus. Remember when you were afraid to leave the Magnet School and go to high school?"

"Yes, but this is different. I don't know anybody."

"You will love it. I feel certain of it."

We continued to reassure her, yet Todd and I did have our own concerns about Brittany's safety. She was brilliant, but sometimes her inattention and her deep concentration caused her to be totally unaware of her surroundings. Those surroundings, too, would be very near where Kathy had been kidnapped and killed.

A few weeks before the semester was set to begin, Todd's doubts were recurring.

"I don't know, Debbie. Why couldn't we wait until next year, when Katelyn will be there on campus with her? I'm not anxious about how she'll do in her classes. I know she won't have problems with any of the work. I'm just nervous about her crossing the street by herself."

I laughed, but I knew he had a point.

Brittany popped her head around the corner of the den and said, "Daddy, I'll be fine. You don't trust me?"

"It's not at all that I don't trust you. I just know how you can zone out sometimes."

"Zoning out" was a term Brittany used when she said ADHD was getting the best of her. Four years earlier, when she was entering high school, we'd thought it was time to include her in all individual education planning meetings, so she could better understand her disabilities and take part in decisions. Until then we'd never emphasized any of her diagnoses out of concern that she would feel less capable than the other students. She'd known at an early age that she couldn't write legibly, but we'd just told her that with her writing issues she needed to type so others would be able to read what she'd written. From then on, we were straightforward with her about ADHD, dysgraphia, and autism spectrum disorder.

"How about this," Todd went on. "We arrange your schedule so that you only have to go to buildings bunched together on the same side of the street."

"Seriously, though," I said, laughing. "The week before school starts, we'll go to the counseling center and talk with someone about classroom accommodations."

"I don't think I need accommodations anymore, Mama. Did you know that everyone on campus is allowed to use a computer?"

"Yes, but I still think it's a good idea to let them know about your dysgraphia in case you have to complete forms by hand or fill in a bubble sheet for a test."

"I guess you're right."

When we visited, we were pleasantly surprised by the university's willingness to create an accommodation plan for Brittany. The administrators would proceed to contact each of her teachers within the week. Also, this would be the only meeting I would attend with her. Throughout the rest of her college experience, she took on that responsibility herself and made sure she pre-submitted her schedule to the center every term.

After the tour, and after we'd walked the whole route of her schedule several times, she grinned at me and said, "I've got this, Mom."

I battled worry that first semester, of course, but whenever my mind would go to thoughts about "what might happen," I sought to remember that God is in control and that His plan is always perfect. And I would reflect on the words of Jesus in Matthew 6—the same ones Todd and I had discussed all the way back when making decisions about expanding our family:

> Do not worry about your life, what you will eat or drink; or about your body, what you will wear. Is not life more than food, and the body more than clothes? Look at the birds of the air; they do not sow or reap or store away in barns, and yet your heavenly Father feeds them. Are you not much more valuable than they? Can any one of you by worrying add a single hour to your life? And why do you worry about clothes? See how the flowers of the field grow. They do not labor or spin.

> Yet I tell you that not even Solomon in all his splendor was dressed like one of these.... The pagans run after all these things, and your heavenly Father knows that you need them. But seek first his kingdom and his righteousness, and all these things will be given to you as well. Therefore do not worry about tomorrow, for tomorrow will worry about itself. Each day has enough trouble of its own. (vv. 25–29; 32–34 niv)

The Lord not only had protected Brittany throughout her childhood and adolescence, He also had abundantly blessed her with, among other gifts, a sharp mind, a wealth of creativity, a quick wit, and a stunning imagination that overshadowed all disabilities. Whenever fear tried to get the best of me, I would think on how He'd been with us through every diagnosis, every trial—every single moment—and how it was He who had marked out a purpose for her life that would be revealed in His timing.

After she'd completed several weeks of the first term, we all realized that Brittany had found her niche in college. She came home telling us how she joined in on discussions and enjoyed the intellectual conversations between classmates. The year flew by, and each term she was on the Dean's list with a perfect grade point average.

The following summer Katelyn graduated in the top of her high school class, and in the fall, began as an undergraduate, on a full scholarship too. As she had done her whole school career, she tried to mother her older sister. But suddenly, this time, her older sister was having none of it.

"Brittany, when you finish your class at noon, come to my classroom and wait outside the door until I finish, and then we'll go get something to eat."

"No, I'm going to wait for you in the Student Center."

"You don't need to go there by yourself."

"I've been going there by myself for over a year. I think I'll be just fine."

Katelyn began to see that her role was changing—and it was changing in a good way. She could step into the shoes she'd been born to wear, those made for "little sis."

Brittany became more and more independent and loved every minute of it. She shone with a zest for living; she was like a flower blooming in fast motion. She fit in with classmates—so many of them now took notes on laptops. She was no longer singled out, and she found each day exhilarating. She thirsted for knowledge; university life seemed both to quench and to fuel it. She'd come indescribably far since the days of echoing phrases, collecting acorns alone, and avoiding social interaction.

Throughout her time in college, Brittany talked openly about her autism and other disabilities. When asked by a professor to provide a signature on a form or other document, she would joke, "I can write it, but you probably won't be able to read it." She'd learned not only to accept her differences but also to embrace them.

"Mama, do you think someone can grow out of being autistic?"

"I don't think one grows out of it. But you yourself are an example of how one can overcome difficulties and challenges associated with it. Why do you ask?"

"I'm not sure. I guess that's true. I actually think a couple of my professors might be autistic—if they are, then they didn't grow out of it. And I like being autistic—it gives me a childlike spirit. I don't want to be like everybody else."

I laughed. "When you and Katelyn were little, I remember the two of you singing the Peter Pan song "I Won't Grow Up" a million times."

"I really don't want to grow up."

"I hate to tell you this, but you are grown up. That

doesn't mean you have to lose any of your uniqueness, though. You are a beautiful, mature young woman, and God has given you many abilities you can use for Him."

After four years, Brittany graduated with honors, having earned a degree in English with a minor in French. Immediately she applied for graduate school, was accepted, and received several scholarships to continue her English studies. She enrolled and began in August, anticipating another great year. We didn't know it then, but just a few weeks later, in October, there would be another diagnosis—one that would turn out to be the most frightening of all.

Chapter Twelve

It was one of the first cool, brisk days of fall, and Brittany was excited about the approach of Halloween. As a child she had loved dressing up, and while she now was a college sophomore, this still was a fun opportunity to dress up in costume without being considered weird.

Late in the evening, though, after Todd and I had gone to bed, she came into our room and woke us. She was crying.

I sat up from a dead sleep. "What's happened, Britt?" Something seemed terribly wrong. She'd always had a high tolerance for pain, and she never cried.

"I don't know. I'm sad."

Todd had sat up too. "What are you sad about?"

"I don't know."

"Well, something must be wrong. Were you thinking about something sad? Did you watch something sad on TV?"

"No. I just started feeling sad."

Brittany had been on medication for anxiety since starting high school, but this didn't seem like anxiety. Nothing we said seemed to have any effect. She cried throughout the night, simply inconsolable.

No matter how we tried, we couldn't help her with the overwhelming feelings of sadness, and the next day I took her to the doctor. She was diagnosed with depression, specifically seasonal affective disorder (SAD), with which I'd been entirely unfamiliar. The doctor prescribed a medication and suggested we use light therapy.

"This is the worst thing I've faced in my entire life, Mama. If I didn't have Jesus to help me, I don't think I could handle this."

"He will be here for you, just like He has been since you were born. We carried you home from the hospital, not knowing what each day would hold, but we knew God was with us and would always be there for us. You know He has promised never to leave us or forsake us."

Morning after morning I would go into her room

hoping to see the bright and cheerful Brittany who usually woke with a song. But each day it was the same—she was depressed. This hardly could have been more different from her normal disposition. Practical jokes were her specialty, and how I longed to go back to the time she'd put the rubber band around the sprayer in the kitchen sink, even if I'd gotten drenched when I turned the water on to wash my hands.

She'd always been the entertainment when our family got together. Now, instead, her sadness seemed to consume all the oxygen in the room as she entered. I tried, and failed, to comprehend how someone with such a joyous disposition could be moved from happiness to sadness in such a short period of time. I hadn't known, until I started reading about depression, that it can have genetic influences. Over the years, several members of our family have suffered from certain forms of the illness.

"Mama, I just want to be myself. I hate feeling like this. Why do you think God is allowing me to feel this way?"

"What I know is that there will be times when we won't understand the reasons why. During these, we can seek to draw close to Him, and He will be there for us."

"I feel like He's far away. That's the hardest part. I want to feel near Him, but I don't."

We prayed each night. Weeks and weeks would pass before she began feeling like herself again.

Brittany would struggle with depression, off and on, the whole time she was in graduate school, always leaning on God for her needs. One night she wrote this letter to express her feelings.

> *Dear Depression,*
>
> *I remember when you first plucked me from my happiness. I was in a state. I wanted God to help me, so I prayed for him to break me and show me the way home. Then you came. I know God allowed you into my life for a purpose, but those were the worst months of my life. I felt alone and worthless. You whispered to me that I was a sinner, unworthy of God. You reminded me of how I continually fell to temptation and of all my failure. I was in a black pit and couldn't get out.*
>
> *I remember the tears, the pain, the sadness. I felt that I would never come out of that anguish. Through it all, though, God was with me. He gave me verses and devotions and His voice was continually fighting with mine. You, depression, were a test of my faith. God showed me, through you, that I needed to be stronger in Him. He gave me*

His words, His songs, and His love. I gradually came out of the pit and into the light, but I knew that really it was always there and He was always there. You thought you were stronger than me and I did too. God showed me I was wrong. He showed me that I was weak alone, but with Him all things are possible. He showed me that I am so loved, by my family and my church friends, and by Him above all.

You do not own me and I am free of your chains. You are always lurking, but God can sweep you away. I still feel bad at times, but God keeps me singing. I will always be in His hands. Satan can throw you at me all he wants but HE WILL NOT WIN. I thought I was dead in you, but I was alive in God and still am. And guess what? I always will be.

God's Child,
Brittany

Throughout the months she continued to write as an outlet for her emotions about living with depression and as a way to wage war with symptoms of the illness. She wrote a number of journal entries and poems including the following:

For a long time now I've been living with a monster inside. I experience this black beast, depression, as a darkness that feels unshakable, a darkness millions of others likewise know all too well. Its voice reminds, again and again, of all the mistakes you've made; it says you're worthless... pointless... hopeless. Sometimes it brings sadness. Other times it just leaves me numb.

Even so, every time I've fought this fiend, I've always known deep down that God is with me. Sometimes it's hard to feel Him there—sometimes I feel entirely alone—but I know the truth all the same. The truth is, darkness doesn't stand a chance against God.

God is light; because He's given me His Spirit, light never leaves me, no matter what my eyes see, or think they see. If you've encountered extreme physical darkness, you've probably also seen how even a bit of light creates a stark difference. The source of light itself doesn't merely encroach upon darkness: Light crushes the night.

Thinking on this, some time ago, inspired me to write a poem about my experiences:

I Will Stand

I'm Bending
But just see if I'll break
If you think you own me that's your mistake
Because I am strong
And God's been with me long before you came

You sneak
And you claw your way in
Look at me with your Cheshire grin
But God is stronger than anything you'll throw my way
All the stuff you say, telling me I'm less than

Telling me I'm flawed, broken, not worth the breath in my lungs
But that's God's breath He gave me
And when He made me He said, "You are loved"
When you toss your words like weapons, He tosses back

Loved, priceless, covered with His blood
He covered my life in a changing flood
Looked at me saying "My Son makes you worthy"
And you dare say I'm nothing?
I am a child of the King

Oh there'll be days when you creep up
But I know when times get rough He's there
And I'll carry on with my Jesus light
Cause the smallest bit can crush the night
So you… will… fail

So run off with your tail between your legs
Back to the dregs of filth from whence you came
Cause I can tell you in Jesus' name
You will crumble, I will not stumble
On His rock I will stand

Brittany receiving her diploma

During grad school, while taking classes, Brittany worked as a graduate assistant in the university's English department. Her main job was to help undergraduates with writing assignments and with editing their papers. My child, who used to need to be asked a question in order to speak, was asking other students questions about their written papers. My child, who can't write legibly, was typing out notes to help other students revise their work.

She would graduate with a Master's Degree in English. Todd and I were, and are, so proud of her accomplishments.

One of the worst conditions for someone who fights depression and contends with autism is to lack a routine. When Brittany finished graduate school, we prayed she would find a job that would add structure to her daily life. We prayed that God would open a door through which she could put her considerable talents to work. After much prayer, He laid it on her heart to write her first book.

We set up an office right across from her bedroom, where she once spent hours alone consumed by thoughts that only she knew about. Now she would sit for hours at her desk consumed by thoughts about how to open herself to others. She would write about her experiences of a loving God blessing her life immeasurably with unconditional love, and of how throughout the many battles she's fought He has helped her to stand and endure and emerge victorious. She titled her first book *Blessed Assurance: Finding Refuge in the Father,* and it was published in March 2019.

Further, God opened the door for her to work for our local newspaper. She currently is there as a reporter; her work appears weekly. She also plans to take her driver's test later this year.

No matter how much I've ever worried that diagnoses and syndromes would define her, they don't—God does. She is His child, a gift whom we offer back to Him, with the prayer that He will use her to reach others for Him through the words she writes and the life she lives.

As the saying goes, while we don't know what the future will hold for Brittany, we do know who holds her future. By the Lord's definition and ours, she definitely is no ordinary child—she is extraordinary!

A Note from Brittany

FROM A YOUNG age I knew I was different, though perhaps not why. I was a quiet child and preferred my own world to the company of others. I enjoyed my imagination and always was ready to set off on the next make-believe adventure.

In later elementary school, I became aware that I had dysgraphia and ADHD. But my parents didn't dwell on my disabilities, so I didn't either. I didn't focus on being different and being disabled didn't worry me; I was just me.

I likewise think a lot of good came out of it all. Because of ADHD, I frequently became obsessed with one topic or another for long periods of time.

History was one such interest; I would fixate and then delve deeper and deeper into people and events and eras and learn all I could. I likewise believe ADHD played a key role in my love for reading, allowing me to immerse for hours on end with my nose in a book.

As I drew closer to high school, I learned I had pervasive developmental disorder as well. I began to understand how its traits affected me, and I realized that I seemed to develop more slowly than others my age. I haven't seen this as a bad thing either. Among other effects, autism has allowed me to continue to embrace my inner child, to remain young at heart. (I continue to collect dolls just like when I was little.) There's an innocence to this that usually is left behind during or after one's teenage years.

My disabilities also have been a benefit to me in my relationship with Christ. He calls us to have a childlike faith, and a youthful spirit has helped me to continue, and grow in my faith, seeing through a child's eyes as I seek to forgive others, love my enemies, and show kindness to all. I like to look for the good in people, just as I search for good in the trials I face.

Through various diagnoses and afflictions, I've learned more and more the significance of relying on God in *everything*. This is especially true of my experiences with depression. I've had to lean on Him, day by day and moment to moment, while standing and warring against the darkness.

Amid the difficulties I have been blessed to meet new people, see new places, and enjoy incomparable experiences. In God's strength, I count on challenges to keep shaping me into a stronger, more well-rounded person. While disabilities are not my identity, I believe that God has used them, and will keep using them, to bring out the best in me.

No Ordinary Child

Brittany

Excerpt from
Blessed Assurance:
"Fighting the Good Fight"

As we journey through life, we come across mountaintops, places of happiness. We feel confident, as if nothing can shake us. Everything seems as it should be.

But as happy as those special times may be, every one of us, at some point, will find ourselves on a downward slope into a valley. It might be gradual; it may be like a quick tumble. Valleys are filled with disappointments, with sorrows, and with battles we feel we can't fight.

I've had quite a few of these downturns. I tend to try to fight my way out, and when I do, I just fall flat. I end up curled into a ball, thinking, Woe is me—there's no way I can do this.

When I have this attitude, though, I'm overlooking something very important. God is stronger than any opponent, with more than enough strength for any battle I may face. He always has what we need; if we're willing to humble ourselves, leaning on Him and asking for His direction, we will find it.

God also gives us himself—we can listen to and speak directly with Him. He will grant us wisdom and the strength of His Word, the help of friends and family, and the ability to walk whatever path lies ahead. In the valley, we may feel like there's no way we can triumph, but through Him we *can*.

When life has you down, never give up. Instead of wasting time and energy on self-pity, look up. Get up, put on His armor, and stand your ground. Nothing can tear down what God lifts up.

Afterword

FOR MANY YEARS, my responsibilities as an Induction Coordinator included providing professional development to new teachers. During presentations I discussed characteristics of ADHD, dysgraphia, and autism to aid their understanding of how to accommodate for individual differences among their students. I was able to speak from firsthand experience because my daughter had been diagnosed with and lived with these disabilities.

One facet of my approach was to include statistics for children diagnosed with autism spectrum disorder. When I first took that job in 2001, the ratio of children born with autism was 1 in 150. For 2019, the

CDC has estimated the ratio at 1 in 59. Having recognized that more and more families will be raising children who are on that spectrum, I wanted to tell Brittany's story to encourage parents and to share that while they will be confronting certain hardships, the triumphs absolutely can far outweigh the trials.

Every year of Brittany's life we have celebrated her accomplishments no matter how great or small. Whether it was learning to ride a bike at ten or winning a poetry contest in high school, we understood how essential it was for our daughter to realize that she should never give up seeking to reach her goals. In May 2016, as I watched her walk across the stage to receive her diploma for earning a master's degree in English, I knew she had learned that lesson well, and I knew it was imperative that we endeavor to share it with others.

Every one of us is unique in God's eyes, and He will use both our abilities and our disabilities for His glory if we'll allow Him to work in our lives. The perfection He has promised us is coming—in heaven, though, not here on earth. The apostle Paul asked the Lord three times to remove what he called his "thorn in the flesh," yet each time God answered that His grace is sufficient (see 2 Corinthians 12:7–10). These words apply to us too: His grace is all we need, both in the hardest of times and in all others. Even if disabilities are such thorns, just like the thorns on a rose bush they're surrounded by immeasurable beauty, and they bring joy to the lives of everybody around them.

Relying on God is the most important thing we can do. The ability and willingness to call on Him can give us the peace and comfort we need in any circumstance. He loves us so much that He sent His only Son to die and then resurrected Him so that we might have eternal life if we will repent of our sin, believe in Him, and make Him Lord of our lives.

Through some of my toughest times, the Lord has shown me that His ways are always, always better than mine. After finding my sister's killer twenty-five years following her death, my plan was for him to stand trial for her murder. God's design was different, and justice was served without a lengthy trial that, among other things, would have been very difficult for my family. Anytime I'm asked to autograph my book *Sweet Scent of Justice*, I write, "God's plan is always perfect" above my signature.

Back when my husband, Todd, and I were dating, we spent many evenings sitting in an old swing in the backyard, looking up at the stars, dreaming about getting married and having children. Our aims did not include having a child who one day would be diagnosed with autism. God had a better blueprint, and by His design we were blessed with a lovely, intelligent, and talented child who has showed us in countless ways that people aren't defined by a label.

> "I know the plans I have for you," says the Lord. "They are plans for good and not for disaster, to give you a future and a hope" (Jeremiah 29:11 nlt).

Whenever Brittany stands before the congregation at church to sing a solo, writes a wonderful poem, or makes us laugh (and keeps us laughing) with her wit, I am reminded that God's plan and desires for me and for my child are flawless.

Photos

The first time I was able to hold Brittany in the Neonatal Intensive Care Unit.

Brittany a few days after we brought her home from the hospital.

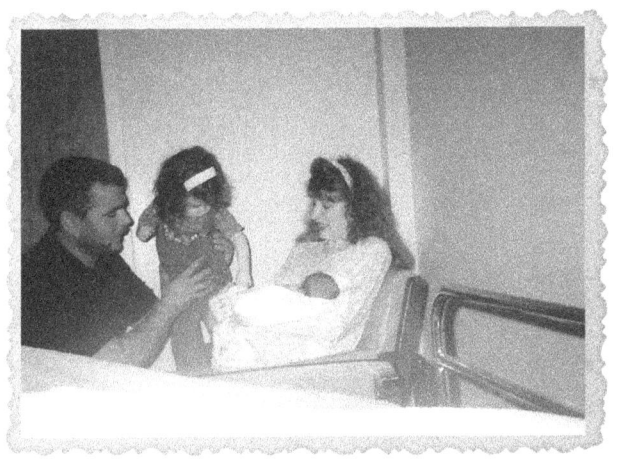

My sister Amy holding Katelyn and showing Brittany her little sister for the first time.

Grandpa Wilson reading to Brittany when she was about 8 months old. Her passion for reading started early.

Brittany banging on the piano when she was around 15 months old. She always did love music.

Brittany rocking in her little chair. She loved to sit in it and watch her Mother Goose rhymes tape.

Brittany listening intently while I read her a book.

Brittany pretending to play the piano and singing with Katelyn and her cousin, Jodi.

Brittany around four years of age playing with Katelyn and her cousins Jessica and Ashley

Brittany in a pretend wedding dress when she was in kindergarten. Dressing up was one of her favorite things to do.

Brittany's first grade picture. She loved going to school to learn.

Brittany enjoyed playing with her dolls.

Brittany around 7 years old with Katelyn and cousins Bradi, Jodi, and Nolan

Brittany playing when she was in the 2nd grade.

Brittany when she was around six years old. Our family always had a strong faith in God. From an early age she and Katelyn learned how to pray.

Brittany having a tea party with some of the girls in the bubble.

Brittany with her sister Katelyn when she was about 11 years old.

Brittany with her cousins, sister, and the girls in the bubble on Halloween

Brittany around 12 years old with Katelyn posing in their dance suits.

Brittany receiving a writing award when she was 12 years old.

Brittany around 12 years old with some of the girls in the bubble (Tinsley, Bailey, Bradi, Jodi, Katelyn, Meredith, and Caroline). She took dance with them for nine years.

Brittany at 16 with the girls in the bubble. They went for a fancy dinner for her Birthday.

Brittany at 17 with Jami, her resource teacher.

Brittany receiving flowers from her Grandma Wilson at her first Rose Theatre Play. Doing these shows really helped bring her out of her shell.

Brittany at 17 with her sister Katelyn and Katelyn's future husband Taylor.

Brittany in the 10th grade with Katelyn and Taylor.

Brittany during her freshman year of college with Katelyn and Taylor. In college she learned to socialize more and made new friends.

Brittany when she was 23 at the American Girl Doll Store in New York. She's been collecting American Girl Dolls since she was in Jr. High.

Brittany at age 27 with all of her cousins and their families.

Brittany at her book signing with Katelyn in 2018. She is excited to have published her first book, Blessed Assurance: Finding Refuge in the Father and hopes to publish more in the future.

Acknowledgments

So many people have played a part in helping Brittany become the person she is today.

Here I would like to thank:

My husband, who is my rock and the one God designed just for me to be the perfect daddy in every way.

Katelyn, who for so many years played the part of "big" sister to help Brittany overcome many of her daily hardships. God gifted you with an abundance of love and patience, and your daddy and I thank Him for you always.

Taylor, who treats Brittany like a little sister that he pesters but protects. We prayed for a Godly spouse for Katelyn, and he blessed us with you.

Our family—her grandparents, uncles, aunts, and cousins who have always loved Brittany unconditionally.

Sandy, a second mother to Brittany. There are no words to express how thankful we are to you for everything you did as a friend and teacher to help our child.

The girls inside the bubble: Meredith, Karoline, Tinsley, Madison, Baylie, Jodi, and Bradi, for making Brittany's childhood one of the best possible.

Jami, for being a friend as well as a teacher to Britt. The humor that you shared with her helped her through many difficult circumstances during her school days.

Jett, Veronica, Morgan, and Amy, for bringing out the best in our daughter through your teaching.

Melissa, not only the best occupational therapist but also a good friend. There is no doubt that God placed you in our lives, and we will be forever grateful for all you did for our daughter.

Melissa and Brittany during a therapy session

About the Author

Debbie A. Wilson, author of *Sweet Scent of Justice* and *Even in the Valley*, has been an educator for more than three decades. She holds undergraduate and master's degrees in elementary education and her certification in administration and supervision. Debbie has been married to Todd, her high school sweetheart, for over thirty years, and they have two beautiful daughters, Brittany and Katelyn.

www.ingramcontent.com/pod-product-compliance
Lightning Source LLC
LaVergne TN
LVHW041622070426
835507LV00008B/401